POETRY NOW

MIDLANDS

1993

Edited by Pat Wilson

First published in Great Britain in 1993 by
POETRY NOW
4 Hythegate, Werrington,
Peterborough, PE4 7ZP

FOREWORD

Although we are a nation of poetry writers we are accused of not reading poetry and not buying poetry books: after many years of listening to the incessant gripes of poetry publishers, I can only assume that the books they publish, in general, are books that most people do not want to read.

Poetry should not be obscure, introverted, and as cryptic as a crossword puzzle: it is the poet's duty to reach out and embrace the world.

The world owes the poet nothing and we should not be expected to dig and delve into a rambling discourse searching for some inner meaning.

The reason we write poetry (and almost all of us do) is because we want to communicate: an ideal; an idea; or a specific feeling. Poetry is as essential in communication, as a letter; a radio; a telephone, and the main criteria for selecting the poems in this anthology is very simple: they communicate.

Faced with hundreds of poems and a limited amount of space the task of choosing the final poems is difficult and as editor one has to try to be as detached as possible - quite often editors can become a barrier in the writer-reader exchange - acting as go between, making the connection, not censoring because of personal taste.

In this volume around one hundred and ninety poems are presented to the reader for their enjoyment. The subject matter is as varied as the writers themselves, love, hate, war, peace, the seasons, etc.

The poetry is written on all levels; the simple and the complex both having their own appeal.

The success of this collection, and all previous Poetry Now anthologies, relies on the fact that there are as many individual readers as there are writers, and in the diversity of styles, subjects, and forms there really is something to please, excite, and hopefully, inspire everyone who reads the book.

This is a book that is a representative collection of poetry as it is being written today: POETRY NOW.

Contents

For you

For you I would dream dreams of gigantic proportion
Half hidden in the clouds of the future.

For you I would plunge to the depths of the ocean
For coral and spangled shells
To adorn you.

For you I would fight dragons
Returned singed and burning
To beg for your approval.

For you I would build a castle
From my blood and shining tears
And furnish it with my bones.

For you I would grow gardens of flowers
To surround your dreams with sweet fragrances
While you softly sleep.

For you I would walk naked
Through Arctic snow or dry desert heat
Simply to amuse you.

All these things I would do for you
My child
My yet unborn child.

Ruth E Watkins

The Chair Lift

Yes, I have loosed the bonds of all-restraining earth,
And 'danced' the tree-tops high into the cloud.
Upward I've swept and swayed, in silence held
And felt the mist like fingers, singing loud
I've raced the wind and snowflake through the day;
I've watched the tracks beneath, and known the way.

Silence all around, its unseen presence felt,
        And touched, and heard; its pulses known.
Tall trees, like sentinels beneath the peak they guard,
        Their branches bowed and burdened as they frown
In strength and might at minute, feeble, Man -
Soaring, swinging, high above all space.
My heart leaps up and loathes the very pace of worldly life.

The trees, now ghosts and blurred -
Their tops reach up, but never find their goal -
Nought can despoil this sanctity, this space;
Only the lines, criss-crossed, together race
Into unknown, unguessed at, peace.

And now the run - the rush of wind and body
Sway against the whiteness, reaching out
To find a solitude, a peace, a grace.
A great expanse of white, then trees
Search out, and grasp the sun, like night
To blot out day. Dappled patches swish
Along the route; a turn, a jump, a run -
Crouched low, as though in flight.
        Twisting, turning, now in freedom driven
        To part the trees and shadows 'til a riven
        Path shows clear. And then, at last,
        The open slopes again. The last run home.

Sybil T Chapman

2

The Factory

The building stands forlorn, neglected,
Twisted metal and crumbling brick.
The watcher gazes, alone, dejected,
While through his mind the memories tick.
A once proud factory, machinery churning,
Clamour of voices and steel on steel.
Columns pounding, pin-wheels turning,
Even today it still seems real.
But the watcher knows it is only a dream,
That silence hangs like a festering sore
And the factory which had been his life
Like he himself would work no more.
No pain, no anger is in his mind
Just a deep sorrow that this should be
The only monument left behind.
Marking the death of a community.

Winifred Blackham

Hobbies

When you paint a model aeroplane
The time goes whizzing by
You stick the bits together,
But you'll never see it fly.

When you switch on the computer
And you twiddle all the knobs,
Your homework gets forgotten,
And so do all the jobs.

You can do a jig-saw puzzle
Every evening if it pleases.
The picture's looking lovely
But you've lost the final pieces.

What about a pretty tapestry,
Until you get cross-eyed.
You'll never see the same again
Although it's magnified.

A train set's always lots of fun
If you have got the knack.
The engine races round and round
Then rattles off the track.

You can plant a thousand daffodils
Outside the kitchen door.
Though you've waited all the winter
All you'll ever see is four.

Oh, the joy of gentle hobbies
Sets new challenges to meet.
I'm off to do a bungi jump
Before I get cold feet!

Linda J Foster

The Peacock

The peacock is a very proud bird
and shows off to everyone
Feathers of blue, black, gold and green,
glistening in the sun.

Strutting around in stately grandeur,
with full plumage on display.
Each feather preened with splendour
and unfurled in colourful array.

God's creation portraying such beauty
there is nothing that can compare.
Each feather designed by the Master's hand
with a beauty so rich and so rare.

Teressa Rhoden

Love, Temptation and Fear

The sweetness of a smile
The temptation of a kiss
The pain of love I feel
As I sit with tight clenched fist.

My tears of pain are with me
To soothe my lonely nights
In them I find my refuge
They always win the fight.

Unable to voice my fears
I sit here in the dark
I sit and watch the time go by
Until I hear the morning lark.

The sound of a car in the roadway
The sound of a plane in the air
As I drift into a fitful sleep
I tell myself someone must care.

In the morning I wake up exhausted
To go on with my life as before
But I find as the days drag on
I miss you more and more.

But I must go on with my life
Miss you as I do.
When someone asks who it is I love
My answer will always be you.

Esther Liggins

Ecstasy

I watch from my window
A girl walking swiftly down the street
Dressed in black - her skirt ending at the curve of her bottom.

A short, smart haircut for her black hair;
Slender legs in black stockings; a low cut blouse.
She is bent on pleasure and eager to enter adult life
And find new experiences.

Her parents wave to her, praying silently that she will be safe.
They are Churchgoers, you know,
And not really au fait with discos.
They know only the old dances.

Their worried eyes follow her
As she is swallowed up by the bend in the road.
She does not look back.
They have told her to be careful but are willing her not to go.

They move back into the house
Telling each other that their daughter will be safe.
They watch television with fear clutching at their hearts.
They watch the clock, willing her to return.

Another couple, a few doors away
Still wait up for their daughter.
She also walked away eagerly -
Her death made the headlines in the newspaper next day.

Giggling nervously she swallowed drugs
And they killed her.
Her parents wait for her still by their window.

Dorothy Minten

Cyclone in the Ghostland

Dripping down the trickling oilslick of night
Drifts closer, swallows up the asthmatic light
As the city slowly doses off to the industrial lullaby
A single pre-adolescent prayer drifts in the smoky sky
An innocent trying to find meaning
An infant trying to find direction
In the confusion of rejection

In this world so soiled and wounded
In the souls so closed and blinded
In her frail torn ear, stamped by a scarred hand
Hiding in her mind, afraid she'll never understand
On the skyline, there's a cyclone in this ghostland
A parental embrace in this orphaned place
Splinters of a promise, after the sky falls
And trembling nails her heart to a thousand walls
Above the city in the dreams
So many lambs wonder on a mountain top blade
Longing blindly but sickeningly afraid

So easy to lose your path in this twilight
When millions of candysticks catch your sight
And your heart and throat clutch tight
And you hunger so, but try to fight

And the cyclones coming
See all the sheep start running

Pray in the shadow and still stand
For truth and meaning in this ghostland
The seams are splitting to the tumultuous tune
And the cyclones coming very soon . . .

Jessie Jukes

The Legacy

When amid life's hustle and bustle
Do people really give much thought
About the way the earth is changing
And all the battles to be fought?

Not the ones involving weapons
Guns and missiles not required
Just a thoughtful and caring heart
To stop this earth from getting tired.

All the demands we're putting on it
Depriving it of greenery
Destroying vital oxygen
And devastating the scenery.

The pollution from the factories
The lorries and the cars
The chemicals and gases
The fault can only be ours.

Start saving and conserving
Water and energy
Don't leave it all to someone else
It concerns both you and me.

For if we do not heed the warning
Start making provision now
We won't have anything to leave
So let us all make a vow.

We would like to seal for our children
A healthy and happy fate
But isn't it our duty to offer them
The *same Legacy*, if it's not too late!

June Scrimgeour

Undesirable Situation

Stay indoors, scar-felt, numb, non-entity.

Strive for perfection please.
Pleasing no-one all the time.
It seems you are surplus to requirements, superfluous,
and all this time is suddenly on your hands.
The seconds drip like water-torture and command you
to please yourself with pleasant thoughts;
a glass of wine in a dry, faceless desert.
Happy with knowledge.
Not knowing the day you stand in
or the week you lived in.

It left and left nothing except repetition
and doing the same thing. It's all the same
to stay mildly content with have-nots
and dreaming of distance in centimetres.

When a mile can be walked in less than a year
this brings hope,
for every mile walked is an achievement.

Richard Bocock

Untitled

I hold you
With all the strength
Of an open hand.

The fear of you slipping
Through my fingers,
Delicately balanced
On the soft banks of flesh,
Against the fear of crushing you
(Beneath my thumb?).

Twisted arm behind my back,
Hidden,
My nails silently scar my palm
As trust clutches fear
And soothes her to stillness.
Bird heart beating
In clenched breast.

You hold me
Caught fast within your grip.
But the bruises,
Purple prints upon my pale body,
I inflict.

Rachel ffield

Storm

Calmly tides turn - moon motivated
Sensually curved, rising and falling gently
teasing the beckoning shore.
Touching the sandy earth, leaving slowly
gently quenching the hot grains.

Frothed fingers reach out to hold on -
the sand slips out of reach.
Water drawn away, gently rhythmic in her folds.
Washing over the helpless beach.

Mood changes, fierce she becomes
Demon-possessed, lashes against the shore
Tranquil blue to jealous green
Torrid, tormented, the monster's core.

Tossing, tumbling in frenzied claims.
She smashes - helplessly writhing
The waves flow faster, blurred
Howling with the wind.

Suddenly, she retreats slowly away
Retreating from the thirst-quenched sand
Lapping gently, distanced and recoiling
From the stranger's hand.

Kate Steadman

Miracle of Spring

A swallow flew back today.
From the searing heat of a wild shore,
Where winter passed.
Over earth scorched brown and bare,
Soaring high over forests and seas,
Islands beneath,
A swallow returned.
Northwards to your temperate nesting, resting place,
The clear fresh morning air of spring,
Gentle primroses 'neath powdery willow puffs
Warmed by a precocious sun.
Dewdrops glossing the leaf tips,
Glistening the grass blades,
Vapour misting roadways,
Welcoming swallows.
Build your muddy home high on the beam,
Close by bursting life on hedge and tree,
Emerald green to burnished yellow.
Dappled shade near stream
Bubbling and rippling over satin stones.
A single swallow, exhausted iridescence,
Resting on high, swaying wire.
I saw you as I passed below and, for an instant,
Everything stood still,
A Rembrandt of nature, framed for eternity
In memory. Time slowed, giving precious moments
For thought and thanks
For one small miracle, a swallow's return.

Ruth Chapman

Quietly Insane

Scarlet-red sunset - grown old; dark dotted
     Mold breeds on brush which paints heavens of clay.
     Lights melting might doth drain away with day.
Solar scolded sky heals, thus seals rotted
End of filled bright time. Gaped mouth is clotted,
     Clogged with blanket of blackness; yet on't tended
     Teeths' twinkles are enhanced - for dark is here, light is hid,
Is hid, and undercover, evil plans are plotted.

Our tortured minds, like sky, go through transition.
In a trance, the dead send their transmission.
And our sane thoughts, learned taughts, find their dismission.
We seek in night great cover when safe-sane coalition
Can break. It breaks and meets, greets madness. Us all
Have sane-up and sane-down like day hath sunset and sunfall.

Rich Sears

14

Back Home

Gone with the winds, fathers free,
  Spirits once entombed
    in bodies like thee,
      Left behind sorrow
        that's plain to see,
          But joy in their hearts
            for this Heavenly key.

Gary Lanham

Autumn Departure

Brittle leaves fill the floor,
Frame the space
Your footsteps left

They are a carpet of colour,
A brown red river,
Flying and flouncing to a stop,

A flow that turns to ice
When the wind falls
And my heartbeats slow.

That is where you stood
As the golden skies grew dark
And your eyes were dark

And my heart turned dark,
That is where you, still,
Reminded me of a statue

Disturbing the moonlight and
Wrecking the horizon
I can no longer see.

You filled me first with desperation,
Then a fury and then tears,
And then, in a swirl of leaves

You were gone with the sunset
And the summer and your silhouette,
And I am left darkling.

Brittle leaves fill the floor,
Frame the space
Your footsteps left.

I try to pick them up but
They fall, disintegrate in my hands,
An ashen breeze, like your love.

James Barker

Midnight

Midnight leaps from the townhall clock
Hurling echoes at silent roofs.
Cats' eyes glow in sounding dark
Kestrels stir in the ageing tower.

Shadows flirt with the tick of the clock
Chiding the hours at dead of night.
Moonbeams shimmer on skylight worlds
Chasing tails of chimneypot mice.

Urban foxes steal through the night
Silently padding endless miles.
Yelps spring sharp from back alley bins
While scrounging tastes from tables of man.

Here and there as the clock ticks on
Figures sprawl in guttery filth.
Stray dogs tear at putrid clothes
At midnight, midnight, midnight, midnight.

Screech owls swoop, alley cats prowl
Milk bottles totter down in a heap,
Rattling glass on ringing cobbles
Reflecting the light of a paling moon.

Midnight, midnight, midnight.
Jousting hour of the ghouls.
Midnight, midnight, midnight
Bewitching hour of the souls.

Midnight . . . midnight . . . midnight . . .

Evelyn Wilkins

The Gallery

The street is grey, dull and crude,
then I see her rising up, a white vision, sacred,
the mirage in a desert of noise.
The heavy oak doors sigh as I struggle in from the
endless stretch of bodies,
that are Birmingham.
Silence reigns on the insurmountable marble staircase,
and the air is still
as I pass into the first gallery, I am immersed in colour,
texture and light.
In awe I glide from one painting to the next,
overcome by the richness of each,
unable to digest one before greedily searching for another.
From room from to room I pass,
the pictures become blurred,
my mind is racing,
my legs protest,
I am gorged and yet hungry for more.
The gallery is cold and still,
yet I am burning with colours, passion, and expectation.
I've been everywhere but seen nothing,
the hours have slipped away,
while I have devoured each piece.
Reluctantly I pass back out through the doors.
I am engulfed into the intoxicating mass,
my body is here but my soul remains there.

Claire Bassett

Dead Stop

Proud, aloof, stood the man,
alone and quiet on the stony beach.
From where he was standing,
he could see the great pulley wheels of the mine,
stark against the greying sky.
Stopped. Dead. Frozen forever.
They'd stopped only days before,
come grinding to a definitive end.
But the people, real people,
who'd worked there,
still existed,
were still there,
still feeling, hurting,
their pride and dignity smashed and torn,
as though their lives and struggles, and them as people,
were meaningless nothings.
The man picked up a stone and smashed it into the crashing ocean,
to be devoured and forgotten by the tireless destroying waves.
The fight left in him was whisked away as he stumbled up
the rocky cliff-face,
walking into the narrow streets with barely an attempt at dignity,
and bright posters not yet torn from walls mocked him,
'*coal not dole*' and the others,
stood out with ironic defiance.
As darkness descended on the nation,
the ex-workers lay sleepless and scared in their homes,
until sleep came and they too had been devoured and forgotten.
And they lay asleep, their existence secure,
But their lives,
Stopped. Dead. Frozen forever.

Steven Bassett (15)

Heed the Warning

'The time has come,' the Earth did say,
'To give me back my life,
The humans are all killing me
And devastation's rife.

'How dare they go on plundering
And taking what is mine.
My resources are not plentiful.
I must give them a sign.

'So come on Moon, come on Sun,
Help me. Play your part.
We need them to take notice.
Global warming's a good start!

'I'm dying on the surface ,
I'm dying underground,
I'm dying up above me,
All those chemicals around.

'I gave them land to live on,
I gave them air to breath.
I gave them rivers, seas and forests.
Everything they need.

'So why do they not realise
It's getting far too late?
Nothing lasts forever.
How much longer must I wait?'

Paul Fisher

Van Gogh Paints Sunflowers

The cold black fluid of Death
Stirs to give Light.
The light of Numinous Sight
Ignites Vincent's Mind,
Activates his brain,
Rendering his hand, his brush, his knife
Animate.

. . . Dark Canvass . . .
. . . Rugged, rude strokes of form . . .
. . . Green and Gold Mosaic . . .
Impasto boldly ventures
Into sculpture's dimensions:
Petals carved in paint.

Dazzling realisation;
The Sun's brilliance
Blinds Vincent of its Presence.

. . . Spectral Canvass . . .
. . . Living Colour . . .
. . . Creation recreated:
Dazzling Realisation;
The Sunflowers' Brilliance
Is Creation's Presence.

. . . Living Canvas of Colour . . .
Fragment of Creation
Is one with the Sunflowers.

Immortal Masterpiece
Is one with Vincent's God.

Haydn G Greenway

Beginnings

Invites posted
party hosted
exploits boasted.

Eyes meet glancing
heart beat dancing
intrigue chancing.

Twosome leaving
hardly breathing
new dawn nearing.

Val Howell

The Lovers

She smiled his way in snowdrop time
With winter on the wane
Her dainty step and features fine
Made him her love-sick swain.

Crocuses in groups and drift
Gave the lovers' hearts a lift
Through April's swift capricious showers
Heading for primrose covered bowers.

The words he uttered so heartfelt
Had tulips nodding in assent
With bluebells misty and replete
A scented carpet for their feet.

The hills criss-crossed with daffodils
Their hearts suffused with thrills
They entered nature's wonderland
And found their hopes fulfilled.

When roses in profusion bloomed
And clematis climbed high
Their hearts were perfectly in tune
They vowed the knot to tie.

Finding an ivy-covered church
A benediction to their search
Dappled sunshine, light and shade
Illuminated man and maid.
With vows exchanged and golden band
They pledged their future hand in hand.

On honeysuckle-scented nights
With owls aloft in silent flight
With arms entwined, they sleep and dream
Their love, their vows are evergreen.

Albert Robinson

Seasons of my Love

Shy spring is here, with myriad green,
On hedge and tree lies dewdrop's sheen:
So sweet and gentle, kind is she,
Springtime is my love to me.

Now here comes summer - radiant, fair,
With shimmering colours in sun-gold hair,
So bountiful and rich her reign,
The summer's aye my love's domain.

Autumn arrives in red and gold,
The world in ripeness now behold,
She gives her all in lush array,
The fall is, truly, my love's day.

Crisp and freezing, winter's here,
Snow and Ice I never fear,
For, 'twas on a winter's day
That my true-love came my way.

Seasons come and go apace,
In each I see my true-love's face,
The years go by, time marches on -
My love and I remain as one.

M J de'Vandré

26

The Gift

The gift that is precious
Is the gift
That is chosen with care,
Endless hours of thought,
Hours spent in shops
Looking for something
That exactly matches
That person's particular taste,
Or the gift that is home-made,
Like a cake, or the gifts
That the children make at school,
Sticky with an excess of glue,
But put together
With so much care, patience,
And infinite labour,
Not to mention the agony
Of keeping 'it' secret.
Or the friend who spends
Countless hours recording
Some special piece of music,
Or who looks for a book,
That will delight,
For the time of a busy person,
Is the most expensive item,
That they can be given,
Since it is an offering
Of themselves.

Jane Nyman

I am Like a Caged Bird

I am like a caged bird,
Who once wished to be free,
Confined and locked in a prison
That you had made for me,
But now that you have gone away,
And left my door a-jar,
I find I only want to fly
To where I know you are.

I am like a caged bird
Hopeless if loosed to the wild,
Unable to stretch my wings and fly,
A dependant and fragile child.
Now that I'm free to wander,
And mix with the birds of the air,
I find no contentment in freedom,
It's vast and it's lonely out there.

Confine me again like the caged bird,
Like the caged bird I used to be,
For if being without you is freedom,
Then I don't ever want to be free.

Robert Houghton

Escaleene (Rise and Grow)

Be unperturbed.
Be not this sadness of mine.
Bubble with your person from within
to outside.

I believe in freedom, Yet!
I want to chain the love and ease
right by my side.
With these selfish thoughts
I'm a little blind.

I've been in the cold
for so very long,
I knew some day we would stumble on.

Nourish now the thoughts divine,
Flourish now as we climb,
The seed of love we sow in dream,
Will give out warmth
She'll Escaleene.

Bill Bradley

Life

Looking at life,
It's like a map, with diversions everywhere
It goes through lanes and tunnels
With obstacles here and there
Along these roads we travel
No time to stop and stare
We go along until we come
To corners we must turn
But what we'll find, I do not know
Or even why we're there!
The answer surely lies with God,
So through the power of prayer
I will ask and He will show me
The path I have to take
Where like a butterfly from its chrysalis
In His garden I'll awake.

K Toovey

Life

Like the sands of time we drift from day to day
Taking with us the memories of our yesterday
Sift out the bad from the good and thrust it out to sea
'Life' is good to us, my friend.
'Life' is good to me.

See the rising of the sun on a summer morn
Our world will brighten up again - another day is born
But if a shadow clouds your day, be patient and you'll see
That 'life' is good to us, my friend
Think of times to be.

When nightmares pound the brain, there's confusion and despair
And Oh! The sweat and tears, this 'life' you cannot bear
But awaking from this nightmare, worry not - you'll see
That 'life' is good to us, my friend
And once again you're free.

Time heals the wounds that never show
Like a drop of blood on the pure white snow
Think not of the past, but of times to be
For 'life' is good to us, my friend
Believe in destiny.

When the sky is burning and there's a stillness all around
There is a gentle peacefulness, the wind makes not a sound
Side by side we'll wander from the woodlands to the sea.
Oh! 'Life' is good to us, my friend
And you are good to me.

Be bitter not at thy fellow men, even though they stare
For they cannot help the way they are - of love they're not aware
Some loves may live and some may die - but there is eternity
'Life' is good to us, my friend
One day you will see.

Jacqueline P Butler

Forever Friends

(Dedicated to Helen Hale)

The sands of time roll by
friends are but a few,
Special thoughts of someone dear
Sincere and oh so true.

You've seen me through bad times
been there through thick and thin
'Thankyou' hardly seems enough
My head was in a spin.

You pulled me through all that
Showed you really care
No truer friend I've ever had
You made the time to spare.

I'll never forget all you've done
the kindness you bestowed
Where would I be today
If compassion hadn't showed.

Lin Ellis

The Concrete Jungle

People gaze with awe, at proud stately homes,
Well-kept country manors, and mansions rare.
Pray come with me to our city
To see the concrete jungle there.

Absent are the green fields
Nor, flowering gardens to share.
But we have tower blocks, and terraced units,
Do come and visit, if you dare.

Like a dark foreboding sentinel
Those multi-storey blocks do stand.
Once so much needed, yet a blot,
Upon this pleasant land.

Proud authority, in our city halls,
Control, design and plan,
Those awful concrete boxes
To house the working man.

See the multi storey car-parks,
Vast concrete, shopping centres too.
With concrete, over and under pass,
to allow mere humans through.

Of concrete you will have had your fill
No more will you wish to see.
You can retreat back to your mansion
and leave the concrete jungle to posterity.

Thomas Gillen

Eternal Flame

See the light through yonder window?
It is the light of youth.
I have passed through that light
bathed in its glory;
Danced and twirled between its flickering
flame.

I have been taken by its heat
To the highest of my passions;
And thrown through its spitting sparks
To the lowest of my deeds.
I have tasted the sweetness of its
hot lingering breath;
Burning my throat and suffocating my eyes.

I was blinded by its beauty.

I still am.

Roseanne Shorthall

My Telephone

Thank God for me telephone
Me means of communication
It helps me in so many ways
In many a situation
I'd sooner have me 'phone
Than sit and watch the tele'
'A up' the bell's ringing
'Hello' it's aunty Nelly
'How are you today?'
O I aint been well at all
I went out yesterday
And had a blooming fall
I don't know what happened
I'm careful as a rule
But when I fell upon me bum
I didn't half feel a fool
A man rushed over to me
And said, 'I'll help you if I can'
I said, 'Oh thankyou very much'
You're a very nice man
A very very nice man
Now don't get laughing
I know I'm a fool
But nobody will change me
Me sense of humour never goes cool
I think I'll be like aunty Nelly
But I don't want to fall
You never know
With a bit of luck
I might meet a nice man and all.

Eileen Budd

Illusion

Oh, it's so beautiful in here,
I'm always happy . . . what's to fear.
And I've got lots of friends who come,
even stay with me when day is done.
It's nice to be a popular child,
and not one of those who run so wild.
Here my friends come . . . what games we play,
hopscotch and Mr Wolf . . . we are so gay.
They bring me presents . . . chocolate and blooms,
my favourite biscuits, and bonnets with plumes.
We jump in the pool, and watch the fountain play
and little Sally cut her knee today,
I wiped dry her tears, and we sat to pray,
and thanked our sweet Jesus for this happy day.
Oh, it's so beautiful here . . . I never cry,
I'll always be a child . . . not grow old and die.
We'll go to the sea tomorrow, all in the van,
and collect shells and starfish wherever we can,
then we'll have candyfloss and ice-cream,
and huddle in bed, and share in one dream.

'The old girl's still up,' the warden said,
'About time we drugged her and put her to bed.'
'It's a shame,' said her partner, 'been here fifty years.'
'Well I'm off from this nut home . . . must clean the furs.'
They both looked at her sitting there, in her padded cell,
'Poor old girl, must be hell.'
'She's a vegetable you know . . . always has been
mind's completely blank . . . like sleep without a dream . . . '

Belinda Freeman

A Pavement Plea

Hungry and homeless, lonely and cold
None are spared whether young or old
Where is the society we all should share
What price is paid when the system lacks care
Do we walk on
Ignore the pavement pleas
Must the poor and the destitute
Stay without shelter and freeze
Why do some have and others not
We who complain whatever our lot
How we take for granted warmth and food
Think of these people, the anonymous brood
Offer to help the many without
Make an effort to do something about
The situation, the tragic state
The poverty trap, it cannot wait
Do not ignore
Do not walk past
Stand and gaze down on the floor
Put aside greed and class
See others as yourself
Extend a hand, take the time
Forget your own need and wealth
Look beyond the grime
Beneath the skin we are all the same
But the division of haves and have nots
Remains cause for shame.

Marie J Owen

Returning

Have you seen the hills by moonlight as the train goes rushing by?
Here and there a gleam of water, then a glimpse of mystic sky.
Have you heard the quiet voices calling from the ancient trees,
You belong here, why not stay here, call the softly rustling leaves.

Did you see the woods below you, branches reaching from the dales,
All unchanging, ever stretching, whispering memories, telling tales
Of those young and joyful happenings, of those dreams all still
                                                              untold;
This the country that has nursed you, calls you back into the fold.

Oh! you've lived by seas and cities and the years have swiftly gone,
Come back to the beautiful hills again and the place where you
                                                              belong.
Back to the valley that loves you, back to the scenes of old,
It's time to return to your home again and for longer tales to be told.

Margaret Chatham

Untitled

Temptation first arrives
in the form of a wild
   dream
With slow rampant witness
to depraved death
and bloody horse running
with desire.
The strangled circus freak
alone in town
for just one winter eve

The first guest arrives
as a fleet
of screaming ghosts
and wolves

now enter the Queen
With steady fragrance ripe.

- And all is welcomed
   and forgot.

Ross McNeill

Fall and Rise

Waste land town
to waste land city
to waste land pity
Coloured gasometers thrust upwards
Reaching the sky
Leaving behind dereliction
Euphoric celebration
Over terminal decay
Economic culture burns once more
Rushing, the train
Flying, the 'plane
Vibrancy the life
Avenging its discourse
Avenging the disunity
Avenging for growth.

G Probert

Perceive

my
chair
sits there
I see it
and move
to sit
on it
but once seated
it's invisible
deleted.

Mick Humpage

The Light of Arthur

Cool darkness shadows field and forest, hill and valley;
wrapping them about in the shroud of death's dark cloak.
Grain and tree, bush and flower, each lie sleeping,
with promise keeping: to awaken soon, to awaken soon.

Cold hearts hide the spark of fire, the fire of life, the life of light.
Yet dawn approaches; light awakens, sparking fire back into life.
Lancing shafts of inspiration; pure awareness fills the land.
Radiant light against the darkness has power to stay death's heavy
hand.

Awake! Rejoice! The light is born! again from out the womb of death.
The golden orb; the light of Arthur. Awake! Rejoice the radiant birth!
Newly born the young sun rises, weak at first but growing strong.
Fed by the spirit of his father; nourished by magic's song.

Within us all his light re-kindle. Guard it well and help it grow.
Make all shadows now to dwindle, replaced by light's increasing
glow.
In after-times cold limbs begin to stir, dreamily awake from sleep,
with light infused into the land, leaf and branch their promise keep.

Paul D Pritchard

Greensleeves

She's not a water nymph or faerie queen
Huddled in her anorak and jeans
More concrete scenes than these she has surveyed
Of dusty bricks and walls without a seam
Away from where the willow tree has swayed.

Her feet encased in leather, grass and mud
A vague attraction almost stirs her blood
Uprooted from the river bank she frowns
And stumbles down to where the water tugs
And laps against the wet and muddy ground.

She does not make the leap with dignity
To reach the green and mossy rock she sees
But guesses where uncertain feet should land
Unbalanced now, has grazed a denim knee
But jumps again, out further from the bank.

With water ringing in her eyes and ears
And willows tugging at her tangled hair
On dappled granite rock she sits, confused
And trails her hand in waters crystal clear
Her Sony Walkman, pocketed, unused.

And in this sunlit, isolated lair
That weathered rocks and rippled waters share
Although her feet are wet and hands are cold
She deeply breathes a breath of scented air
And finds there is contentment in her soul.

Helen J Baty

A Mother Reminiscing

I seems like only yesterday
That you were just a tot
With your pretty little golden curls
You sat there in your cot

It only seems a short time
Since you used to laugh and play
And I often have to smile
At the funny things you'd say

And now you are a woman
Oh how the years have flown
And I just can't believe
That you've got children of your own

I hope they make you happy
Just the same as you made me
Because you're still a little girl
Locked in my memory.

Elizabeth M Price

I Myself

What is this elusive state I long for?
Is it real? Is it close by?
That tantalising glimpse I sometimes see
Is it reality or,
That I would desire it to appear so?

My days spent in purposeless day dreaming.
Leading a life I resent,
To exist in a conventional world.
First I need to find myself,
Then take courage and follow my vision.

At last, with my open eyes I understand
What might still be possible.
To choose the way to pursue to the end.
How wrongly I blamed many things
For the tedious path life had taken.

In the end only I can take control,
Make things happen by myself.
Follow future hopes, forsaking others needs.
So simple the solution,
Will my actions be justified in time?

E M Gilbey

The Bereavement

The young girl, lying face down in the lock,
Has globes for eyes, which contemplate the dark,
And blond hair streaked with weeds that made her struggle,
For this is how she died: in clinging blackness -
The deep cold snatched white bubbles from her lips
To stop them reaching light, with cries for help;
And so she stretched, and rose relaxed and still.
Those eyes will turn to snails before she's found;
Her tongue become a flapping leech, while elvers
Clear as healthy spit, will make their way
Along two parting tendrils, once her legs,
To that pursed mussel, set between slack roots.
She will belong here - gather twigs and slime
On crayfish claws, while sticklebacks and larvae
Fill a womb not used to bearing so much life.

The young girl, lying face down in the lock,
Is not the sweet young thing who loved to boogie.
Her boyfriend, asked to name her, will reject her:
His horny recollections of her hollows
Will smudge with mould, because of this last glimpse;
He'll dream of her and wake up wet and sick -
Recalling how her hands left silver marks,
Like slug trails on his skin, before they kissed;
And yet, with time, he'll see her by the water,
Then she will have a bright, unearthly face
More stirring than the platinum of moonlight;
And he will want her, follow when she calls him:
Sprint to catch her, never getting close
But finding some redemption through his lust -
Because this ghost is beautiful, and human.

Gary Bills

46

I Belong

I am less than a word in life's thesaurus,
not even a twig on Earth's family tree.
My voice is just one in a teeming chorus.
We're playing in destiny's

symphony, rhapsody, lullaby welcome me,
born to the universe shared by our galaxy.
Growing child in a lifetime's fable,
I'm molecule sized in my global

cradle me, Earth mother, gentle of hand
as you warm your brood by daytime star,
and later when blackness grips the land,
take soft silver light, prise the darkness

ajar is a door to a live constellation
of plants and beasts, rhythms and seasons.
There for the loving, this medley creation,
for those who take heed of its rhyme and

reason for being was sought by me
as I travelled the time - miles day after day,
courting religion, philosophy
to find out where the answer

lay down my soul on nature's fertile land,
there to grow and shed it's infancy,
reaching out in one great cyclic plan,
in harmony, placidly, quietly,

humbly now I heed the prophecy.
Wise tribal chief, his flag of truth unfurls
to show the world is not bestowed on me.
Indeed it's proven I belong to her.

Angie Garrett

Urban Strangulation

The worst three words I ever heard,
'West Midlands Conurbation',
Invented by some bureaucrat
With a mental aberration.

Coventry - city of spires,
A place of light and hope,
Exiled from leafy Warwickshire
By some unthinking dope.

He must have been from Birmingham,
That dark, forbidding town,
Not from friendly Coventry -
The jewel in the crown.

One day the city councillors
Will wake - and maybe hear
The citizens of Coventry,
In leafy Warwickshire.

Give us back our county,
Give us back our pride
We're not in the Black Country,
We're in the countryside!

James Blackwell

Signs of Love

Heart symbols cut on bark of beech
once seemed more eloquent than speech.
Initials, also freshly carved,
recorded that two persons loved.

Where are they now, those happy two,
and has time's test of love proved true?
Should either chance to wander here,
would memory induce a tear?

David Hancock

The Bus

The bus slows down
Pausing at the same old stop
To pick up the same old people
Travelling to the same old jobs
Time after time with little relief.
One day I shall get off this bus
And walk away.
One day.

But not today.

Chris Davies

Escape

Oh faded rose of summer last
enfold me in your dewy heart
so I won't see the world its future or past
or times of anguish never to depart

Brush my weary eyelids with petals browning now
like mud dull river eyes from the child
as flies pick with legs of hair along the
nostrils flared from tired sucking from an empty
breast which hangs like a sack from a worn out frame
as she rocks back and forth,
(No-one knows her name).

Yet, Oh faded rose if I stay with you
my eyes like your heart damp with dew
to blur out the world, pretend it's not there
to suckle your nectar with never a care
then the vision will sever the peace which I crave
for with you I will wither and take to my grave
the heart of a coward with no-one to save.

Maureen Westwood

Santa Pause

A lonely croft, on ragged bed
Whimpers from the under fed.
Oh, Santa won't you pause?

In lands so dry, that cannot feed,
The stomachs of the young in need.
Oh, Santa, won't you pause?

A drunken dad, a beaten mom,
No hope for child from either one.
Oh, Santa won't you pause?

This Xmas give to a just cause,
And let our Santa make a pause.

Ernest J Percy

My Memory

My memory has gone quite peculiar.
Events from the past I recall,
But words spoken only a moment ago,
I cannot remember at all.

Now I often forget what the day is,
Or who has just visited me.
I am always mislaying my glasses,
And without them, I simply can't see.

I believe that I know the reason,
Why my memory, it comes and it goes,
Like the sea that rolls up to the shoreline,
Then recedes, as it ebbs and it flows.

Memories are like tumblers of water,
What goes in them first will remain;
But when they are full, it flows over the edge,
And I'm sure that my memory's the same.

Colin A Lycett

Persephone

'Time to get some roses in your cheeks!' my mother cried,
Dragging me from the warm, earth-dark womb
Where I had lived in the arms of my darkly loving love,
To the harsh welcome of the light, blinking and shivering.

Demeter swung her heavy hips and breasts at me
Laughing inordinately, encompassing me with her warm, earthy
                                                          smell,
Crowned with flowers, their petals tangling in her hair,
Pulling me reluctantly into the trembling promise of the world.

Away from the sensual caress of my pomegranate-fleshed Lord -
From the jewelled, heavy breathing richness of his kingdom,
Where I had sat, hung with gold, pale and perfect on my throne.

Was it always like this, this seasonal re-birth,
This shrinking away from change, this painful awakening?

A youth lingers midst the budding trees,
Pale and slight, his hair a primrose cap -
Eyes glance shy promise - his name, Spring.
This hostile world has its seductions too.

B Stanworth

Besotted

As I entered Marks and Spencer's she was browsing through the
ties;
When I walked by a glance gave me large wide apart green eyes.
Lines from Tennyson flew to mind on seeing her standing there,
' . . . a daughter of the Gods, divinely tall
And most divinely fair . . . '
Tall she was, at least five-nine,
Her body slim, legs too; she was a lovely creature
Not more than twenty two?
I couldn't take my eyes off her, attired in expensive charcoal grey;
The figure hugging dress was plain and modest to the knee.
Size twelve, I thought, no more this female so divine;
Nature or God, (Which e'er you choose) has fashioned her so fine.
With head held high and silken strands without a single curl,
Those strands the colour of tawny wine;
Oh what a lovely girl!
High cheek bones to enhance the face with skin so very clear,
A fine straight nose, a fetching smile;
Yes, there's beauty here.
Using little make-up, of powder just a trace;
For no amount of beauty aids seemed needed on that face.
By now my 'Goddess' had moved over to the shirts
And selecting size fifteen,
Had chosen one broad raspberry striped, on background colour
cream,
This she had matched with patterned deep raspberry shade of tie,
And as she paid; gracious! What can he look like? thought I.
She moved and glided to an exit door;
I watched her go and wondered whom the purchases were for?
If she could have had this marked effect on me a middle-aged mum;
just what effect would she have on a middle-aged mother's son?

B Davies

Out of the Fire

Here we go again I thought,
As I stood by frying pan,
Ancestral apes were bad enough
But surely not a mushroom!
That blossomed into man.

Cannibalism suddenly came to mind
And thoughts of eating Frank and
Joe, or maybe George, or even Flo.
Well - I couldn't be unkind.

I pushed away my plate and sighed,
Why can't they leave things as they
were, as Adam suited fine,
And succulent juicy mushrooms
Are a favourite dish of mine.

'Tis true about the stalk then,
I thought, with tongue in cheek,
But thoughts of all those frying pans
Left me feeling rather weak.

But then again I thought,
Could this be all a dream,
That I am me, and you are thee,
And when awake could not we,
An ape, or mushroom be?

Beryl Powles

Remember all

Nuremberg trials, millions gone,
We are not delivered from tragedy yet,
It continues today in many ways,
To us we'd hoped it was a craze.

Easy to forgive but not with facts,
Implanted mines, drawn faces long,
Death by gas, my life, my son,
Gone, not quick, nor forgotten.

Humiliations, demonstrations, outbreak riots
Face to face with willing clones
The facts you should remember clear
You will see the future without fear. .

Nathalie Cooper

Bring Back the Bobby

Oh how sweet
And what a treat
Our joy complete
If we could meet
And warmly greet
Out in the street
Whilst on his beat
And on his feet
In navy neat
To crime delete
A policeman

Why are there none?
Where have they gone?
What have we done
When us they shun
These *Policemen*

Our rates we pay
Thus may we say
That still we pray
PC's should stay
And wend their way
Through streets each day
Their role to play
As *Policemen!*

Horace James

Shroud

From here where the fog
enhances the most ordinary of gardens,
with its swirling silken skirts,
it moves and flows,
erotic.
Like a lover.

Faintly, like a child's small breath,
orange stirs in the distance.
There are three suns,
Bronzing the trees with mellow glow.
If I were a painter I'd paint,
along to the Requiem.

Amber glosses rooftops
and Autumns the trees.
Oh golden landscape.
In this soft focus,
Staggering.
Surreal.

Lisa Hunt

The Threatened Assassin

He'd be on the ground.
And lifting his plain face skyward, there she'd be
Basking in moonglow, with sequins and stars,
Her laugh coloured with shadows, inviting him to sing
                                                amongst rainbows.
But he couldn't, in the straight jacket of his suit,
So I kept him there.
She smiled down on him with postcard precision.
And hand stretched above her head, to grasp my ankles.
Just the way I like it.
So we would take our astral walks,
I her mystical maker, her ideal.
And as I looked deep into her sun sparked eyes
                                                for the last time
I knew that she must dwell for ever, swirling and shining
                                                at my side.

All we left him was her cold, crude, corpse.
So he never faces that way, just stares at my name.
He sees her though, she dusts him twice a week
And we look at him from time to time,
Framed by his frame, by his frame,
above the fireplace,
Suspended,
Just the way I like it.

Emma Goodwin

60

A Good Turn 1933

'I'm going fishing Billy, do you want to come?'
'Yer. I'd luv tew, but I gorra stay wum
Ter look after our kid, cause me mum aye well.
I'll teck the bab for a walk to the Dell.'

'We'll stop and pick bluebells; meck mum feel good,
These days er doe look as well as er should.
There's me dad, e gos down ter the pub for a drink,
But all me mam does is stand at the sink.'

'Er tecks in washin' and gets tew and six a day,
Me gran ses er'll wash er soul right away.
Mum ses the money buys shews - things like that.
Dew yer know what er'd like? Er'd love a new hat.'

'That's funny,' says Tom. 'Only the other day
Mother said she had some hats to give away.
Come walk to the vicarage, see what we can do,
Mother will, surely, have a hat for you.'

'Yo am a good 'un,' said Billy. 'Yo am really swell.
I know a new at will meck mum feel well.'
At the vicarage Tom's mother was soon to oblige,
By finding two hats - both Billy's mum's size.

When Billy's mum saw them she beamed with delight,
And combed back her hair, for it looked a real sight.
Her eyes were a-twinkle, her cheeks went all red,
As a beautiful hat was donned on her head.

'Oh mum, yo look great,' Billy bursted with pride.
'Yo look luvly and fancy, jest like a new bride!'
'I'm better already,' said his mum, all aglow.
'Y'om the best lad a mother could 'ave, yer know.'

Joan Spinks

Untitled

A bud
Nurtured by the elements
dances in the wind, drinks in the rain
Grows
Deep from its roots
searching, growing, growing, searching,
learning
Roots, stem, head - stronger than ever
Soul, heart, whole - alive
Peace
Blossoms a new morning
Greeted by the early chorus
Fresh, open petals welcome it
absorbing, feeding, needing
Its brilliant colour and form
         no longer hidden
For this -
this is a new beginning
full of adventure, good and bad
The future - who knows
But strength will prevail
through rain, wind, snow and love
Ah love - love will live to fight another day
Picked, caressed, standing proud for it's lover
Respecting and living for every part of him
Continuing to do so for days - weeks - years
Kept pressed within his life - never dying
For love this strong never dies
But continues to grow, thrive, for each day
Forever - my love - forever.

Sally-Anne Hawkins

Migraine

I could not stand the noise,
The shouts, the screams, the fears.
I could not stand loud music
It was deafening to my ears.

The brightness from the sun
Really made me blink,
The thudding in my head
I could not even think.

The lines across my eyes
My vision blurred from sight,
When will this pain subside
My head it feels so tight.

The water weeps from my eyes
My eyes feel very sore,
Please let the pain go away
I can't take any more.

Dorothy Jones

The Poet Sniffs a Flower

The amatory poets and troubadours
Rise up in hope, against hope
And issue silent monologues in words of acid emotion
That shatter the thousand desolate days of decay
Leaving a fragmented blackboard of humanity
In which they mark their presence in the falling dust.
Bestowed unto the annals of futures fragile history
When the world is nothing but a void.
Devoid of speech, of light, of sound, of vision
Oblivious to the grief of solitude
The calligraphic smiles of centuries past
Refute the misconceived ideals of human fortitude
To lie unabashed in glorious isolation.
Upon discovery, the incomprehensible stanzas of antiquity
Stand forlorn, encased in the apparel of deceit
A heaven sent exodus of mortality
Confined to the passage of time, and ultimate temptation
Left the quaking earth redundant in fertility
With vampiric desires draining all that remains of tomorrow
In dissension, falling through eventual seasons,
The poet sniffs a flower.

Mark Hughes

The Fantasy of a Pseudo Artist

The lean man starved of glory
Stood before the sober face of the canvas;
One of his paintings spoilt one wall in
His father's house.
He sang to the canary in his cage -
'Seeds of genius are scattered in my brain:
They will sprout from my fingers
And make colours sing;
In my room of masterpieces
I will perch on the highest note.'

Ann Flynn

The Demon Driver

You terrify your passengers with a look of calm upon your face,
Do you perhaps hold a grudge against the human race?

Your foot springs into action at breakneck speed,
You think you are Nigel Mansell indeed,
The car has accelerated to top speed,
This is before second gear you leave!

Your passengers are rigid in their seats with fear,
As you attempt to manoeuvre and then steer,
The car takes off at such a pace,
Unfortunate passengers think they are about to orbit space.

Traffic lights do not exist,
Junctions are a miss, islands you pretend are not there,
Then you arrive at the destination with time to spare,
Pedestrian lives are certainly at risk, cyclists too,
Passengers meanwhile are stuck in their seats like glue!

The journey proceeds in continued terror,
Demon driver never considering he is making an error,
Why are other road users giving me the sign 'V',
Nice of them to acknowledge me,
My driving is perfect anyone can see.

Passengers arrive and now open their eyes,
Amazed that they still live,
But they are frozen in terror, living blocks of ice,
Driver meanwhile, states that the journey was nice!
'Perhaps you would care to come back,' to the passengers he
was heard to say,
'Instead of proceeding on your way?'

'No bloody fear,' they shout as they sprint off into the distance at
great speed.

'Hospitalisation we do not need,
Life is our aim for some time to come,
No more risk taking with your driving chum.'

The driver is aghast,
'What is wrong with them?' he was heard to say,
'I never even got lost on the way.'
The demon survives to drive another day!

Shirley Boyson

The Divorce Settlement

If money can't buy happiness
Then where does that leave me
for I have not a penny left
To lend or spend you see
Should I then be happy
With all that I have not
And never think of all the things
I wish that I had got
If money can't buy happiness
Then what am I to do
I bought the house, I bought the car
Then gave it all to you
Am I not to want for things
That money can provide
Am I to loom in rooms of gloom
And never look outside
If money can't buy happiness
At least I gave it my best shot
I should have used a gun instead
And kept the flaming lot!

Jennifer Jones

That Telephone

That telephone is seducing
My finger,
It wants to whisper nothing
Sweetly, snug on my shoulder.

My uncalled love
For its shy rhyme, rhyme
Is walking above
On the tightrope of a hushed line.

That telephone squats
To outwait my pride,
Feigns death and plots
To tempt my inner-voice outside.

My tingling resentments
Twist around its limp coil,
Convolute emotional experiments
To disconnect the disloyal.

That telephone receives
No compromise.
Tell me what it achieves
Denying even the comfort of lies?

My patience is ringing out
I know what I must do -
Pick it up and with all my clout
Give it a good talking to.

Stephen Clarke

The Word

Words in song and rhyme are the spirit's sails -
Without them we are nothing:
Flotsam and jetsam adrift on the seas:-
An abandoned ship with an untended helm
Lurching in the swell and blown before the breeze;
Or else an ocean liner in mid-voyage
Steering her straight course, no chance to slip away
For fear of postponing the passage. And yet
Who knows what lies beyond the horizon's bounds:
The beauty of the East, or riches of Cathay.

Those who never find them feel no loss - why should they?
They know not what infinite bounds the brain possesses.
The pain and passion of poetry pass they by,
The labyrinths of literature merely confound.
And yet, for those who know the wonder
Of the word and all that words can tell -
Not just in fact, but in life and feeling and thought,
The world expands beyond the bare horizon
And they find in hidden bays the elusive Elysian asphodel.

The sketch becomes a painting,
The simple song a symphony
With layer upon layer of woven sound,
And the plain, passionless paragraph
A demonstration of the harmony,
The beauty and the emotion that is hidden
In the word. Oh, how bleak
Must be the lives of those who know not
What the word can do - how juxtaposition
And euphony can transform rude speech
Into song.

Susan M Bullock

Surreal

'Who cares?'

. . . as the clock rings out it's final warning
knocked to the floor,
                  the alarm shuts off
You mumble, unawake
wanting unconscious back again;
Rolling over, turning away
                  embracing of the timeless state

. . . existence here'll have to wait . . .

No more thinking
                  like injected needles at your conscience
allowing susceptibility to permeate the skin
                  . . . of self assumed immunity.

Irresponsible.

Self induced amnesia
                  . . . mid-thought, mid-sentence
like someone persistently tapping you on the shoulder
                  who you don't want to acknowledge.

Rebelling.

Aching to relieve that constant . . . ticking
                  at the back of your mind;
Conveniently forgetting safety . . .

An immortal humankind.

Not really listening, just blindly nodding
  . . . throwing all else to the night . . .
how close things are . . . forgotten
Once you turn off the light.

Waking to life, a Dali clock . . .
  on the edge of existence.

Stephanie Helen

Gornal Logic

Gornal folk, salt of the earth
Their logic causes others mirth
Foreigners can't think at all
Why they put the pig on the wall
Common sense should tell them why
To see the band go marching by.
Joe was looking tired and pale
Missed the pub, missed his ale
For two weeks he hadn't slept
A barking dog his neighbour kept
His mate, concerned, expression grave
Scratched his head, had a brainwave
Buy the dog, you'll be alright
He'll keep your neighbour awake all night.

Lily I Marsh

Darkness

Darkness is freedom,
None can e'er evade it,
Giving in to all your deep desires,
Wanting to be free,
A heart felt need to be.

Darkness is special,
A place where anybody,
Can escape the real world's lonely drudge,
The scope for dreams to be,
Whatever you desire.

Fingers of darkness,
Entwine their web completely,
Probing deeply through your opened mind,
Offering protection,
Whilst laying in your bed.

Silken sheets are cooling,
They slide against your body,
Giving memories of that gentle touch,
And of how things should be,
If he lay next to thee.

Silken sheets in darkness,
Bring feelings you remember,
Wrapped in comfort, cool yet oh so sweet,
Wanting to be held,
To meet your body's need.

The truth is of darkness,
It is unreal, not normal,
It allows the mind to run its course,
Striving to be free,
Silk sheets, the night and breeze.

But embrace, absorb it,
Never to deny it,
Darkness is the place you want to be,
For in the darkness, darling,
You'll be here with me.

D Hunter

Pilgrim

The sun failed, clouds massed,
the rain washed the dark rock,
Peaks, dominant before,
had now withdrew.
A ceiling spanned the pass,
but not the mind.
The world shrunk. Thought grew.

The wise,
cut and carved and carried
from this place.
Ringed themselves in time and sat within,
ringed themselves in
mystery and lore,
sealed and set before the first Amen.

The wise,
did not seek the woodland
or the sea.
The sword was set in stone and not in sand.
Its drawing came through knowledge
born of light,
and not the lesser power of the hand.

The wise,
sought the solitary
and the rock,
sensing reassurance for their role,
lay within a whisper,
of the mass,
locked, into the strata, and the soul.

Michael Skelding

The Fox

The frost
The winter light
The frozen image
The hunter
The solitary silence
Then the kill -
The glass sheet of water
The open fen
The call of wild fowl
the sensual cries
Of nature
Caught in the cunning eyes
Of the fox.

Roger Thornton

The May-Pole

it runs north south,
icy, history-vault, totem
to fertility, life: death,
re: re-birth. it carries
a time machine, the axle round
which earth: planets: haloes spin.

it garlands greenery,
flowers blossom out youth
sent for the sacrifice into calends
trapped within dark mantillas,
arrows: bull's-eyes: three milky,
billowing layers of thread.

it meets east west,
temples the shadows branching
through Sherwood to all lost,
colonial cultures; a needle
weaving its single moral fabric,
lining it's riches amongst the poor.

it dances finally, pointlessly around
time, is an inquisition battling
its own ghostly preservation
of Muslim: Catholic: Heretic;
for swords run it through, eternally
a scar weeps for La Segunda Natividad.

V Vaughan

Shopping List

Roll up, roll up,
Take your pick
from

Men as:-   little boys
                young blades
                lone wolves
                toy-boys
                free-wheeling bachelors
                misogynists
                menopausal males
                ageing lotharios   and
                sugar-daddies

Roll up, roll up.

Alyson Faye

The Mistake

Winter's fall
Child's born
Mother's in chains
father flew
eyes spectate
While mother tries to fill the plate.
Childs, boy,
Wants the gear.
Mother's down, wants her beer.
Strangers come
Mother smiles.
Figure leaves
I see the tears.

Christopher Jones

Why?

The stark grey desert's wide expanse,
boulder strewn, and cold,
yet hot as fire, and red as blood,
endless, timid, but yet bold.

Jagged mountains touch the sky,
the endless foothills meet
that stark grey desert's wide expanse
with touch so strong, yet fleet.

A river runs down from the hills
and flows to meet the sea,
but at its end is not a mouth
but an old dead, dead, tree.

The storm shook hills reflect the calm,
of the lonely sea, but why,
does a solitary swallow wing
across the rose and violet sky?

Ann-Rebekah Judeh

There is Someone Here

'I've a lady who loves you,' the medium said, 'who would like to
                                                speak to you.'
'Hardly likely,' the man replied. 'My friends are very few,
A lady's love I've never known, my life has been tough and hard,
abandoned as a baby boy in a public house backyard.
I never knew my mother, but lived on booze and wine
and now at the age of forty five I fear the end of the line
is almost on me and I would like you to help me see
if there's any point in going on, any more life for me?'

The medium was silent for quite a time, and tears ran down her face.
She spoke and her voice was changed and unreal,
Reaching through time and space.
The old lady spoke with a young mother's voice,
                                low and full of love.
She said, 'My son, you must go on, yourself you have to prove,
Your mother's condition when she left you, was full of trouble and
                                                        strife.
She prayed and hoped that whoever found you, would give you a
                                                better life.
So be at peace and go from here, and fight life's battles anew.
You can win if you don't give up, my help will see you through.'

On the man's haggard face came a look of relief
like the sun coming out from a cloud.
The first time in his life he'd been given hope
and he wanted to shout it aloud.
He said, 'Tell me more, you have helped me to find, some of the
                                                peace that I seek.
Can I come again, please say I can, what about next week?'
But by now the medium was out of her trance and quietly said,
                                                'Maybe,
Just ring me up and I'll let you know, it is alright, there is no fee.'

The man had gone and the medium was sobbing,
                              tears of anguish and joy,
She was not in a trance and her voice was her own,
Saying, 'Oh my boy, oh my boy, oh my boy.'

Stan Richards

Untitled Work Four

Mother came in from the bathroom,
Her hair was all messy and wet,
She screamed and fell to the carpet,
And closed her eyes to forget.

I was alone in the armchair,
My body and soul far apart,
But I saw it all from the ceiling,
As mother clutched tight to her heart.

I shouted and shouted, 'I'm up here,'
But she lay so still on the floor,
Quiet and shocked her hands closed tight,
Her feet just touching the door.

I stared at her body below me,
The water was gone from her hair,
I cried as I knew she was lifeless,
As I turned, and then she was there.

Oliver L Allen

The Millennium's Child

The second millennium beckons us,
Bearing gifts of both hope and of fear.
We wonder what sort of world lies ahead,
As that time of 'two thousand' draws near.
What lovely, or joyless changes then,
Lie in store for our children's lives?
Is there ought we could contribute, right now,
To ensure, it's their joy which survives?

Review the progress of your life's span
And note how the world has changed.
Wonder with me, if the innovations you see
Reveal a sick world, with its values deranged.
There is nothing amiss in technology's strides,
With its promise of more wonders to come.
Yet there's an ominous sign, in having so much,
If our gain, means our 'neighbours' get none.

The whole world, like yourself, grows more clever,
Though in simple wisdom, we have just failed to grow.
Let's bequeath to the millennium's children,
That one secret, which deep down, we all know.
No material gains, or glittering achievements,
Bring peace or joy to acquisitive lives.
It's in discovering just how to love others,
That the joy of true happiness lies.

Your love and your caring for others,
Teaches all that the future need know.
From love's seed, when shared with all brothers,
The millennium's promised fulfilment will grow.

Ray Lightwood

Winter After Len

The trees have wept their golden leaves
To rivers swelled by autumn rain.
The birds have left their summer nest
To seek the southern sun again.

The wintry winds blow harsh and strong,
Snow blanket sweep to deep white drifts.
Ice candles pend from barren tree limbs.
The frozen land glistens like Yuletide gifts.

But bittersweet beauty of wintry scene
Is lost to one alone again.
Magical season changes nought
And eases not my heartfelt pain.

Without your love I have no eyes
For nature's awesome variance.
I wither like the fallen leaves,
Benumbed, detached and vacuous.

Angela M McHarron

The Recipe for a Happy Marriage

To make a marriage happy,
You need a lot of love,
And all those extra-special things,
That you are dreaming of.
You need a lot of thoughtfulness,
And an understanding heart,
And tolerance and good humour,
Right from the very start.
To make a marriage happy,
You need patience without end,
Sharing life together,
With the loyalty of a friend.
If you blend all these together,
You'll find as man and wife,
That this recipe brings happiness,
Throughout your married life.

Vicki Williams

Untitled

A heartbeat, a kick.
Is that all I am to you?
How can you forbid me the chance;
The chance to grow, to develop,
To become somebody;
Somebody like you?

To feel the heat of the sun,
To smell the scent of flowers,
To hear cries of pain,   .
To taste aspects of life:
It's all I ask.

A heartbeat, a kick.
But one with feelings,
One with hopes,
And no life lain before me
As I've no voice,
No means to protest.

To feel the joys of love,
To see people who care,
To hear the ringing of laughter,
To taste aspects of life;
Is all I ask.

A heartbeat, a kick.
A defenceless human being.
I'm sad that you don't love me,
I'm sad that you don't need me,
I'm sad;
And if I could;
I'd cry.

Joanne Phillips (17)

It's When you Least Expect it

You're no Cinderella,
Would never be charmed to the ball.
But! There is magic,
There is magic!

The Prince; the charming
Home by the stroke of
Dreams come true.

Once I saw a shooting star,
then it was gone.
But I remember the flash
the scrape across the sky.

When asked, have you seen?
The flash and the scrape
across my mind, years on
are with me still.

Yes, I've seen the shooting
star and thrilled,
remembering smile.

Alan Clarke

The Frog

The frog I fear is most queer

he doesn't walk, nor does he talk.

He hops in his slimy cloak,
and all he ever does is croak.

A most unusual chap I'd say,

But if 'Good morning' you should greet, he will most
ignorantly to the pond retreat.

Bonnie Harris (9)

Under Attack

Everything, I cannot see,
empty silence screams at me,
my body, racked with soothing pain,
attacks my senses, kills my brain,
and smashes thoughts I never had.
So sad.
My eyes are stone,
I'm all alone.
A heart of steel, I cannot feel
the pain of arrows raining down
from swirling clouds that wear a frown.
Angry lightening, blackened sky,
vivid sword, a crumbled eye.
Cries of anguish, fill the air.
Inflicted pain. I cannot care.

Stephen J Fellows

92

Childhood

Straining in a bucket
A pudgey grip on the handle
Tiny bloodless fists
To grandpa -
'Off the ground? Off the ground?'
And grandpa -
'Maybe an inch
Yes an inch or so'
Minutes earlier
On his lap
Beneath his pipe
'When I was a youth
Many years ago now
I could pick myself up
Three feet off the ground
And I'll tell you how'

Michael Page

Wear and Tear

Looking and pondering on things that are past,
Knowing and mourning, nothing will last.

Wrinkled and lined, deeply furrowed and brown,
Beaming, smiling faces now wear a perpetual frown.
Greying and fading, shiny, balding patches,
Where tresses once flowed or springy curly thatches.
Knotted and gnarled, great stumps of rotting wood,
Where flourishing elms once majestically stood.
Crumbling and tumbling, once great castle walls,
No longer conceal ancient festivals and balls.
Eroding and corroding, rusting in a ditch,
What was a gleaming carriage, which ferried the rich.
Befriending and depending, folk will always be there,
Suddenly, before we blink, no more memories to share.

Wanting and wishing, that I was so clever,
I could make all we've known go on and on forever.

Jill I Heath

94

The Avant Garden

Eye beg for pardon
In the pristine regime
Of the avant garden.

Iconoclasts of icons cast
Into modernity's machinations,
Eye can't quite see the fascination
With this fraternity's machine-ations.

Eye eye this saga of objet Dada,
De Kooning, Du Champ and long for De La Croix.
Eye feel duty bound to do the rounds
Of this forbidden territory.
But eye want no part of this
Fundamentally mentally funny art.

Eye fail to its sensibility,
Eye fail to see its humanity,
Eye find it hard, but that's just me.

Keith Loines

In my Sleep

When all is still and peaceful,
In the silence of the night,
I hear the sound of broken hearts
Their painful cries and plight.
Funny how time has passed us by,
But I think of you and still I cry.
My tears are silent, for no-one knows,
That inside my heart my love still grows.
I try so hard to block the pain.
With music blasting through my brain.
Aching body wanting you,
To feel the warmth that I once knew.
Mouths that linger and kiss so much,
Your skin so tender to my touch.
Sensations like waves that hit the shore,
Wanting you here, more and more.
As I close my eyes and drift away
You'll visit me again today,
We'll share our love and soon unite,
I'll kiss your lips and hold you tight
But I know you, I cannot keep,
For I'm only with you in my sleep!

Helen Padmore

The Knife

So deep was the cut from that knife,
A cruel blade, honed bright and sharp;
When it came, out of the blue,
That deep dark hue of night
The blow struck, with all its malefic might,
Straight and true to its ignorant mark.

So deep was the cut from that knife,
The stuff of life flowed as a torrent;
Its panic rising, shouting, screaming,
All confusion in the whirlpool whirling:
Pain like the gale of a storm unabating,
Relentlessly ruthless, this merciless agent.

So deep was the cut from that knife,
For a long time it was withdrawing;
Eking out the last dregs of its agonies due
To satiate its thirst, its lust anew,
For thoughtless dominion and selfishness' sake,
Leaving reek and wreck to trail in its wake.

The cut from that knife now long since past,
All's calm, serene, the wound's healed at last,
What's left but a small, thin, lurid white scar:
And yet the cut from that knife's so deep
Inside is a place that festers and boils,
Sometimes to burst forth with wrath and rage,
A hurt no recompense can wholly assuage.

Robert R Smith

To Dianne

Were you then borne just one decade too late?
Ten years too young for me to find in time
For you and I to share our glimpse of fate:
Our common understanding of life's mime.

At first I thought you but a pretty child
A beauty, yes, but young in heart and mind
But then I saw the wise as well as wild
As complex as the course a stream can wind.

One glance from your dark eyes could freeze my soul
Or melt my stern resolve to love no more
To gain from you a smile became my goal
My every foolish thought I would out·pour.

And when at last we danced, not shy or tense
I knew the meaning of the here and now
Your presence overwhelmed my every sense
So warm and vital, Essence of the Tao

Alas it cannot be for you are wed
Sad honour forces me to stay my hand
Were you still free and I still bold instead
I would pursue your love and age be damned!

Peter Shelley-Fisher

Life's Rich Tapestry

A fragile strand of silken thread
each new-born child receives.
On canvas bare, awaiting there,
beneath some ever watchful stare,
each trembling stitch he weaves.

Mistakes cannot be altered,
No dreadful stitch undone.
The cloth remains, complete with stains,
Triumphs, failures, losses, gains,
long after we are gone.

For not a single one is told
what length his thread will be.
Waste not one hour, though sweet or sour,
Consider well, it's in your power
what's left for all to see.

Elizabeth E Smullen

Seasons of Love

Concealed in the mists of time, a boy sat next to a river
watching its crystal waters flow by, meandering into the
distance. Not sure if he possessed enough inner strength to
progress, he seemed contented to merely sit, blissfully
unaware.

A butterfly interrupted the boy's thoughts, fluttering into his
vision. The child, wanting more than a glimpse of beauty, stood
and followed the tiny creature upstream.

The summer sun shone as he revelled in the grandeur that had
enticed him. The animal and plant life blended, producing a
perfect natural harmony. The young man moved further upstream
becoming captivated as gradually the seasons changed.

Akin to the perpetual struggle for supremacy between sun and
moon, Autumn was approaching, casting clouds over the Summer
warmth. A short time later, the beauty he had once known had
deteriorated and become tarnished. As he continued upstream
nature had created a fork in the river. He once more sat, his
mind in turmoil, his mind trying to dispel the suffering in his heart as
he remembered lost paradise.

After a period of despair, the man stood and continued walking,
searching the barren wasteland for the first blooms of spring.

Peter Kent

You

Caught, in a drunken web
Of autumn's weaving.
Scourged by thoughts of love,
Long overdue.
The window traces shadows
On the sunlight,
As I lie in my world
And think of you.

You are the freshening rain after the thunder.
You are the peace, uneasy, after war.
You are the fear that makes me go on living.
The laugh that masks the closing of the door.

You are a summer storm amongst the wild trees,
Forcing an anguished ballet of the leaves.
An autumn evening's golden salutation.
The pattern that a snow-mad fox-cub weaves.

You are the many rainbow hues of living.
You are the sombre, aching, feel of woe.
The dancing joy of Christmas time and giving.
The passing of the days, both fast and slow.

As the days still pass, I do yet struggle,
To break the threads, to hover and be free.
Break from this sunlit web, of autumn's weaving,
The web that ties together you and me.

But autumn dies and soon will come the winter,
As each fresh year a new-born fox-cub finds.
And we, again entrapped in winter's magic,
Will know once more the melding of our minds.

Gerry Ian Massey

Penniless Orphan

The streets are crowded with people like orphan
leaves of trees,
People were busy as bees,
Rushing into the shops for a gift . . . s.
They were covered in blankets,
As there were white snow flakes laid on the ground.
As they rushed into the shop,
Heavenly warm caress touch them.
The smile of a cashier received them with great honour
But I was the one who, who was orphaned today,
Standing in a corner,
Listening to the melodious tune played by accordionist,
Orphan fellow can't give a penny to a penniless accordionist,
To reward his melodious tune.
Thinking about last year,
When I had got enough money to buy gifts,
for all my nearer and dearer,
The only hope . . . hope . . .
I have is just to say a small prayer,
To the Almighty Lord,
As twilight falls,
The street light lit.
They reminded me of the heavenly star,
That had enlightened many years ago in Bethlehem.
The star which has just given hope,
Lifted all mankind from the drain of sin.
The streets are crowded with people like orphan
leaves of trees,
But know . . . now there's hope
For all of us.

Ranjit Singh

Untitled

The wide old staircase (creaking quaintly) leads me down
Past faintly lime-washed walls where, years ago,
Some whitened faces watched, from other centuries,
Descendants climb their way to lofty bed.

I smell the staleness of their lives and feel the
Waves of disapproval and surprise wash over me
As now I swim against the flow and creak my way
Below on such unworthy fangled feet.

The protesting staircase drops me in a lofted hall,
With gaping windows stretched through panelled walls
From darkened floors to yellowed plaster moonscapes,
Now dulled with lifeless light from neon tubes.

A few logs flame in the cavernous mouth of a crested,
Cut-stone hearth (but now no shadows dance).
The organ, veiled in dust, looks on from a minstrel's
Gallery. I laugh . . . but find no echo here.

I walk outside, and cross the gravel carriageway
To find the old church locked, the graveyard full
(The weathered stones unreadable), the tower-clock
Gone . . . I turn, and meet the empty stare

Of glassless windows from the ivy'd stable block,
And watch the driveway vanish into weeds. I find
The walled, once formal gardens now quite overcome
With choking brambles in a yellow avalanche of grass.

A rotting oak leans drunkenly beside an ancient yew.
A score of ravaged apple trees stand locked in planted rows . . .
Who knows what longed-for dreams lie striken here for all to
see,
Beneath the raucous cackle of the crows.

Martin Worster

Pollution

We are the people of Britain,
The scruffiest under the sun,
And strewing the land with litter,
Is jolly holiday fun.

The loos in the service stations
are filthy with tissues and ash,
And stately homes, and national parks,
are ankle deep in trash.

The cardboard mountain is moving,
burying village and town,
The plastic mountain is rolling,
slowly and steadily down.

Irys Wellings

Fish Nessie

Nessie lived above the shop in Main Street
She loved to guess her customers' requirements
'Ah ken whit yer Mammy wants,' she'd say
'And ye can tell her haddock's grand the day.'
Red arms would plunge into the icy barrel
She'd brandish Peter's thumb before your eyes
She wouldn't fob you off with whiting.
Out with her knife, a quick dicht on her apron
Bib-top, canvas, black, tied round with string
Skin and blood and guts in scarce a second
Back-bone stripped, swept neatly down the hole
Fish for the pot, triumphant on the paper.

Ashen-faced, raw-boned, rough skinned, coarse-spoken
She had the knack to make a fiddle sing
Old Scottish airs flew from her fingers
Evening passers-by would stop and listen
Cursing as the rumble of the tram cars
Drowned out the marvel of her lilting music.

One morning Nessie's shutters didn't open
A ten o'clock they broke the door down, entered
Stiffly Nessie sprawled, her brindled perm
Lay cradled in a box of Loch Fyne kippers.
The men stood round in silence, took their caps off.

M M Henderson

And all Because . . .

Carbon-copy couples -
Gaily attired heterosexuality
With clean-cut smiles

Promote saturated fats,
Teeth rotting sugar
And the birth of precocious children.

Cigarettes sold
By the hacking cougher
In the corner of the boozer?

Chocolates made enticing
By a frump in a hairnet
In front of a weepy?

We are what they aren't,
Not what they seem.

Jayson Burns

106

Deception

He climbed up the hill to unloose his kite
A white paper bird in featherless flight
A wind whispered, 'Why be earth-moored?'
Then softly, beguilingly, 'You don't need a cord.'

'You are a bird, all you need is me
Let go of the cord and fly - be free.'
The kite began to peck and soar
The boy could tame his bird no more.

Paper bird answered the wind's persuasion
His life-cord snapped, he succumbed to freedom
But fickle wind grew restless and wild
And returned to the West like a petulant child

No cord, no breeze to take it up, no feathers
Just paper and cane, a frail mosaic
The fingered branches of a tree
Caught it, held it tenderly

Carefully, the boy released it from the tree
'Oh, white paper bird. You can never be free,
Don't you know that to fly perfectly
You need the wind's breath *and* a cord held by me?'

Louise Priest

What is a Child

A child is born, and put in its place.
A cot, a pram, whatever the case.
Drinks milk 'til it's weaned.
And always being cleaned.
Right up 'til it's two
Not much of a clue.
From two to three
Then it's oh deary me
They try us all out
With moods and crying bouts
From four to five.
They become quite alive.
Out and about still trying us out.
They like all their mates
All got different tastes
Some like their bikes
Some like their kites
From five to eleven
They learn about heaven
They go to the shops
With jumps skips and hops.
They go to the schools.
And learn all the rules
From twelve to their teens
They know what life means.
They make all the mistakes
But we wouldn't forsake
This child in our care
Was our little prayer.

Brenda Brownhill

The Friend

We all have those days
When even in the summer time, the mood is blue
When something seems to go amiss with all that you do
Worries loom, there's little to look forward to.
We all know that phase.

Today you feel old
You think 'I'm not exactly cheerful company
So who would want to spend their time with me
To lift the cloud and set my spirit free
Turn grey day to gold?'

There is one who will care
She telephones to say, 'I'm coming over soon.
Why don't we go and do the shops this afternoon?'
She leaves me, laughing, and I start to hum a tune
Just because she is there.

For in the end
It isn't beauty, riches, power or pride
Makes life worth while. It's having someone at your side
To share your dreams. Someone in whom you can confide.
My daughter. My friend.

Ruth Rimell

In Dreams

Every teardrop soft is a thought set free
From this love in bond, my dear, to thee.

Each whispered word a symbol true,
From the poem of life, my love, to you.

Every sign sincere in the yearning breeze,
I bequeath, to you, this love to ease.

While blood flows red in veins of blue
The suffering's long when the wound is new,
My human thoughts engraved in dreams
Are yours forever, dear, it seems.

Jayne Barnfield-Orton

Cat Watching

The cat, she sat a watching,
Could not believe her eyes.

Let me join in, she seemed to say
Looks like a real good time.

We lay in bed, a tangled heap,
Bodies tired and limp.

The cat just sat a watching, and then
She closed her eyes.

Susan B Cresswell

The Eagle is Stranded

Here in your space is where the eagle resides
Watching you with amber eyes
But can you see him between the bars
Or do the curtains shield him from your view
Maybe if you'd let him he'd fly free
Answering the call of the storm in the trees
But you've kept everything in so long
That he no longer knows where he belongs
You've clipped his wings with the edges of your mind
And he looks for the answers to questions he can't find
As he watches the rising moon and the stars in the sky

Sentient and aware, he can hear your voice
The links have fallen and he knows not what you say
All the time he knows he must stay
You give him no choice but to trust your face
So here he remains
Cast adrift in your eyes

Tim Burroughes

Reflections

Such a beautiful sight
a baby's smile
The trusting eyes
of one so small,
>Yet, will that same face,
become distorted by drugs
his mind corrupted
by violence and hate
will the anguish be seen
in his mother's face,
as the one she loves
brings her to disgrace

Such a beautiful world,
being slowly destroyed,
by violence, pollution, racism and noise.

Jacqueline Claire Davies

Lost Love

I take a stroll one Winter's morn
As the moon starts to die, the sun yet to be born
A chill in the air grips my face
As I make my way to my thinking place.

I reach my sanctuary at the canal's side
Scared to face the thoughts from which I cannot hide
From the love that I found, had, then lost
Realising the effect of its terrible cost.

Will I achieve the feeling maybe once more?
The thrill and the joy that burns to the core
Safety, happiness, eternal content
One true emotion that was surely heaven sent.

Will mother luck be watching?
Will a second chance arrive?
When I can escape this tomb and once again come alive
But I cannot see it happening, not tomorrow, not today
I had my one chance and I threw it away.

Now as I accept, the tears flood my eyes
To my hopes and dreams I say my good-byes
I get to my feet, walk to the water's edge
And before I go I make my final pledge
If there is another chance
In another body I can grow
I will grab tight with both arms and never let go.

Yet as I start to sink in both body and soul
A realisation this was my inevitable goal
To be shrouded in darkness and all alone
I die as I have lived
As one
On my own.

David John King

Death of an Image

Archaic, earthly, dispassionate, a slake green slime
Decorates an earthy gorge's jugular scab of stress
Irrevocable disruption scars it's breadth
Canine urine stains, flavoured with the stench of leaves,
Rain, and the erratic plop of aerial secretion.
Depressing, laboured wagons, burden without cause,
Helping pedestrians scrape grit in open sores,
Where delicate brittle skeletons find a temporary grave
Flippant twigs eventually security evoke, to
Crawling, tireless insects, Irish green. And who but
Nature has the heart to forgive man?
And restore itself as though he never existed.
Slowly washing and soothing, breathing
The asthmatic grime of men, then
Cleansing it with the violence of
Unconcerned element, and the inevitability
Of evolution, an image dies.

Ian W Bassett

Rigor Mortis

His eyes are as still
As a thousand dead soldiers.
His mouth is as dry
As the blood around their wounds.
And his heart is as hard
As the bullets that killed them.
And the moisture on his brow
Is as cold as their bones.

As the flies gather round for their banquet of human flesh,
He, the host, has had his fill.
A thousand vacant minds
To feed one ravenous head.
His eyes are still.
His brain is dead.

Sarah Green

Life in the Fast Lane

Twenty four hours
Compressed into ten
Life in the fast lane . . .

Muesli breakfast
No time to fry
Just time to rush
Maybe to die
Life in the fast lane . . .

Appointment 9.30
Coffee eleven
No time to chat
No office banter
Telephones ringing
Fax machines singing
Life in the fast lane . . .

Business lunch calling
Promises broken
Contracts in tatters
Legal eagles descend
Along with the vultures
Fight them or die
Life in the fast lane . . .

Twenty four hours
Compressed into ten.

Deborah Leary

Yesterday's Miner

Off he goes upon his bike, the rattling chain is slack,
The brakes were worn out long ago, there's no light at the back,
His heavy boots upon his feet have got strong steel-capped toes,
And even though he's washed his face, the grime clings fast, and
shows.

With his helmet on his head, he gets into the lift,
Familiar faces going down to start another shift,
Down among the jet black coal, where the sun has never shone,
No natural way of knowing if the day has yet begun.

No sunshine underneath the ground, no twinkling stars or cloud,
Just rock that's wet and shiny black, and men with heads all bowed,
In parts he cannot stand up straight, the roof is far too low,
However much his back might ache - there's no comfort below.

The loyal pit pony passes by, the miner pats his head,
When it's time to have his snap, he'll save a crust for Ned.
The siren goes, his work is done, the miner heads for home,
Thinking of his family - who never hear him moan.

Back home to a nice warm bed, a meal that's piping hot,
A tub of steaming water, tea brewing in the pot,
A fire burning in the grate, patted down with slack,
Reflections dancing round the room, welcoming him back.

Lorraine Brown

118

Breath

Through the . . . Wind, they ran
Toward the Hill, lung's . . . bursting
But they were stopped, still

Defiant voice is
Heard, but hate of King's Dream, gags
Mouth with ball of steel

Oxygen choked tear
Screaming down swollen cheek as
Freedom's heart is burst

No-one can see them
Sniff, short, sharp gasps of air and
S l o w l y . . . gently, seep

A Blood mute, death call
As they die to reap, the breath
That in our . . . Mind, We hold.

Patrick Lane

119

Eight Days too Many

Being Sunday, I really tried
With nerves on edge I could have died
The dinner was but two hours late
and purposely I smashed that plate.

Monday; is there any wonder
the weatherman predicted thunder?
Weather continued in that vein
as washing hung in acid rain.

Tuesday wasn't any better
the day I received that dreadful letter
dog threw-up, vet's bill paid
Johnny didn't make the grade.

Made an effort with Wednesday's cooking
I remember when I was good looking
wore the dress he always hated
husband late and inebriated.

Every day I live in hope
but Thursday I just couldn't cope
frosty morning, car no start
'It's fifty pounds for that spare part.'

Friday all the bills came in
empty purse; weekend looks grim
Supermarket full to choke
Shopping bag handle broke.

The child gave up and ran away
on that depressing Saturday
I took a tablet, the sponge cake sunk
so bought a bottle and proceeded to get
                            incredibly drunk!

Liz Christie

The Has Been

In her heyday she was a dancer.
High kicking, leggy and slim.
She was an outrageous character.
And had a beautiful silky skin.

Her performance was so exquisite.
That, bearing roses by the score.
The men all flocked to the exit.
And hung around the stage door.

Flora never wanted to be a wife.
Since she revelled in the fame.
Florrie Fullard loved her life.
For that was her real name.

As the years rolled on and on.
Flora's limbs began to ache.
She rubbed in cream 'til it was gone.
And more make-up she would cake.

The day came when she was told to, 'rest'
Younger girls then took her place.
Men came no more with fond caress.
No gifts of silk or lace.

She sat at home sad and brooding.
Jealousy filling her heart.
She felt that her life was ending.
In this world she had no part.

In the corner of the churchyard.
Where it could never be seen.
Lies the grave of Florrie Fullard.
Her epitaph, The Dancing Queen.

Jackie Fish

121

Is This the World we Created?

There is love,
And yet there is hate,
There is peace,
And yet there is war,
There is food,
And yet there is hunger,
Is this the world we created?

Richard Ball

The Mountain

It was a peaceful day,
A day as fresh as dawn,
When suddenly it happened,
The mountain was reborn,
It shuddered, it thundered,
It gave a mighty roar,
The mountainside exploded,
That bellowed from the core,
Into a dust filled sky,
Boiling rocks were thrown,
Destroying a village, destroying a town,
Suffocating them with burning ashes,
Spreading for miles around,
Polluting with its poisonous gases,
That settles thickly upon the ground,
All life is destroyed by this force,
For months and years to come,
With clouds of dust setting the course,
Blocking out light from the sun,
But life will always return,
To the land that it knows best,
Hoping that, again it will never burn,
Hoping finally it's lain to rest.

Dean Homer

123

Ecstasy

E ven in these dark damp days when the lees
C ollected from summer's bouquet cloud, cling,
S eep crying in the eaves, and fingers freeze
T o brittle stillness, on each clammy thing
A ttached to the line to dry, I can snatch
S craps of ecstasy from this rummage: sing
Y oung son, sweet page amid the starry watch!

E rode the street grey stone of adult stares,
C ome these soft-footed elves, the Nursery class -
S hepherds in teacloth hoods pedalling wares
T o well-tuned maternal hearts. Hush, they pass,
A ngels tinsel haloed, magi gleaming,
S ongsters huddle, off-key, timeless, en masse.
Y esterday's ecstasy: Were we dreaming?

Claire Smith

Tomorrow Will be Different

Another day, turns into another endless night,
but I've made it, I've survived,
and anyway, tomorrow will be different!

The world wakes up, time I move on
I'm so cold and hungry again,
and anyway, tomorrow will be different!

The daily search for work begins
no home, no job, no job, no home
and anyway, tomorrow will be different!

It's raining today, and my shoes run in,
I've found a warm doorway to sleep in tonight
Oh God, please let tomorrow be different.

Margaret Turley

The Weather

Drip, drip, drip, listen to the rain,
Splashing off the roof and running down the drain,
Drip, drip, drip, all the day long,
Tapping out the rhythm of a sad, little song.

Blow, blow, blow listen to the breeze,
Rattling the door and tossing up the leaves,
Making the trees move to and fro,
Tugging at our clothes and won't let go.

Down it flutters, look at the snow,
Makes it hard to see where to go,
It covers everything in a coat of white,
Oh, but it is a glorious sight!

Now at last, out comes the sun,
Everyone outside, having some fun,
Enjoy it while you can, it may not come again,
Before you know it, back will come the rain.

P V Cox

A Thought Cat

An emptiness of mind I feel,
a page I cannot fill,
an overpowering lassitude
cat-like, invades my will.

Of softest fur a bundle,
limp
and yielding,
like an old cushion.
Dozing before the fire,
sleek, lazy, replete,
with velvet paws tucked under,
somnolent, relaxed,
a cat at rest.

A starling's sudden strident shriek,
insistent, sharp and shrill,
propels her garden-wards
a taut, determined thing,
alert and purposeful
and scenting prey.

Stealthily creeps towards the hoped-for prize,
pauses,
extends a probing paw with claws unsheathed,
tentative, assessing.
Whiskers quiver, sensitive;
the watchful eyes, swift-piercing, see all.
A closer furtive prowl
and then the Pounce.
The Idea is caught;
a poem has been born.

Geraldine Squires

Cancer

That clawing, gnawing, slimy, smut,
That tears at brain and lung and gut,
That gives off acrid pungent smells,
And thrives upon the body cells.

This evil thing in obscene form,
In organs ripped and swelled and torn,
Designs with evil thinking plan,
Destruction of the mortal man.

It sears the mind and roams at will,
Attacking the individual,
United science with monetary might,
Could rid us of this evil blight.

Donald Shaw

The Greatest Pearl

This floating Orb in outer space,
this habitat of human race,
this living sphere, this spectral gem,
this throne of Nature's diadem,
and searching heavens infinite,
no counter world like this in sight,
this speck in universal void,
mans' privilege, on this employed,
crown jewel of our galaxy,
of planets, fairest man can see,
this treasure chest, this pearl of pearls,
a daily glory it unfurls;
rich colour, and variety,
in creatures all, of land and sea,
its wonder, splendour, to discern,
and marvels, man can ever learn;
and man, with sense, and faculty,
with ears to hear, and eyes to see,
here wealth abundant, to sustain,
and beauty, that will entertain,
provision full, for man to share,
if man will for his neighbour care,
partaker of this global wealth,
he must preserve its global health!

Arthur George Carter

Disciple

Your catwalk views certainly look the part
In their branded new dress,
A second, deceptive layer to a heart

Which lies dormant, an impenetrable
Clothes rack of opinions,
Smothered in ill-fitting hand-me-downs, sable,

Tailored to impress like pleas from a
Dead repentant sinner,
You shrouded no-hoper, genius groper,

Interloper. Strutting in that fashion,
Parading shamelessly
Borrowed garments, scissored legs and needled arms

Like a drug addict, proud of your torpor.
'Passionless heroine,
The latest trend is suicide,' I whisper.

David Ellerton

Seagull

On Christmas Eve I saw a seagull wheeling
Over the rooftops - gliding, plumage gleaming,
Over the heated, foetid stores, the shoppers
Clutching, shrewd-eyed, their calculating purses -
Over the ugly streams of screaming traffic,
Like some archangel over hell - then distance
Received him past my straining sight - my seagull.

It was enough - some fragment of that day
Redeemed for me, freely, unknowingly.
Cool images flocked then - grey waste of waters
Swinging beside a wide, deserted shore;
Dark seaweed, tide-intoxicated, lifted
From listlessness to swaying forest, sinking
To sleep with the ebb-tide, rooted in rock;
Pools in their secret hollows, microcosms
Of the vast ocean - undisturbed, unseen
Until the next transforming tide; winds sweeping
Wildly across the bay; waves rising, racing,
Pounding the naked shore, and seagulls sailing
Along the wind, and calling endlessly.

And suddenly the city resembled a bauble -
A hollow, spun-glass, mindless, meaningless thing,
With its heat and glitter and calculating purses,
The smiles denied in the eyes, the forced good-will.
Something I found in a wheeling seagull's wing,
When I watched him over the rooftops, gliding, gleaming,
And received his gift - a vision of swinging waters,
Wide beaches, cold and still.

Winifred Mustoe

Fields of War

The long forgotten graveyards,
Of where the soldiers live,
Tells the greatest story of their lives,
And everything they did.

The flowers above all the graves,
Tells that they are not forgotten.
Their souls are still in the shade,
But are not downtrodden.

The sad sirens still ring in the air,
The homes in gardens still do stand,
Of when the enemy was still there,
And of dirt on a coffin did land.

Their families still weep for them,
Of when they lived at home.
The only memories that now live,
Are their photo's all alone.

Charlotte Round

132

The Factory

Floating around
intoxicating liquids,
a purple haze
now a blind vision.

Turn it on
that fucking television,
just got in from work
and my tea's in the oven.

Think I'll go up the pub
just for a change,
I've read The Mail
but nothing's changed.

Great goal last night
that's what I just heard,
taking another sip out of my pint,
Mustn't drink too much
or else I'll be late,
my job starts at 6.30
and finishes at 5.00,
my clock card's quite bent
and my mate's had the boot,
shit, it's Tuesday I've spent my wage.

Intoxicating liquids
a purple haze,
now a blind vision
my life hasn't changed.

Peter Quentin Francis

Lost Love

You stand upon the shore of time
Like waves thoughts come and go
Dreaming of wind in your hair
Emotions you are afraid to show
You find yourself lost and alone
Sweet moments from the past
But like the whispers on the breeze
Those memories will not last.

Martyn D Jones

A Gentle Summer Evening

The blue sky pales to a softer hue.
Flowery clouds ease across above me.
Cheery sounds of bowlers bantering behind the wall.
The July sun pushes its last arrows of light toward the hedge;
Slight shivers of an evening breeze bathe my forehead as I sit
                                                        motionless
And remember such simple feelings some fifty years ago.
My ears attune themselves to sounds:
Sweeping swallows go screaming by, a blackbird's muted
Staccato warning of danger in the hedgerow chair beneath.
A woodpigeon murmurs its contentment, calm in some thick
                                            high foliage.
A jet plane needles the air far above, its tunnel sound
              struggling incessantly to catch up.
Pods of laburnum hang limpid above the lawn
Shrivelled, like dried-up peas waiting to be freed.
Swallows, like tiny black axes, throw themselves through whisps
                        of cloud with frenetic intent:
And now another day is spent.

Arnold Alcock

Untitled

There once was a lost thought,
Buzzing, creating havoc around my head
Until it flew
Right out of the window.
I opened the window, of course,
In the hope it would be released.
I now keep the window closed
Just in case it may fly back in.
Open windows make me nervous,
But seem essential at times.

Linda T Moseley

Dance

A gallows sun wrings moisture
from a garden already choked
and flung aside by wet the beds,
vinegar leaves,
and vermin sycamore.

Grandfather soft-shoes by, trowel
in hand, to tend lost beds of sweet
summer fruit. A shuffle only
Grandmother knew.
Intent upon a more

contemporary stage, a
ring of burnt, apple-pie faces
fails to clock his secret passing.
Fails to hear his
weight fall through the couch grass.

We, spellbound, rapture seizing
our curious hearts, feast our eyes
upon the last dance of a trapped
wasp. Spotlit by
a magnifying glass.

W

Seasons

The Earth is waking from her sleep
As distant church bells ring,
The rain is falling gently,
The season?
It is Spring.

Summertime quickly follows,
With long, hot sunny days,
Cloudless, clear blue skies,
Touched by the sun's golden rays.

Autumn turns the leaves
from green to red and brown,
Silently they fall,
Onto the frosty ground.

Cold and dormant lies the earth
As nothing stirs within her,
Fresh and deep is the snow,
The season?
It is Winter.

D J Allen

The Sentence

'I'm innocent,' the young lad cried
As he left the court for a cell.
The Judge said, 'You have been fairly tried
As far as I can tell.'

Down the steps the lad did go
Escorted by a Cop,
'Think yourself lucky, lad,' he said,
'They no longer do the drop.'

After five long years behind iron bars,
The lad launched an appeal,
With more sifting of new evidence
Which no-one would reveal.

The lad was left in jail to sweat
Silently cursing the law,
Still protesting his innocence
As he paced the small cell floor.

The lad was locked up for ten more years
When more evidence came to light,
And judge and jury had to admit
All along the lad was right.

The lad, of course, was now a man
And bitter as can be,
But rejoiced with family and friends
The day he was set free.

This story has a moral
Never judge unless you're sure,
For the locking away of an innocent lad
Causes heartaches no doctor can cure.

Marjorie Floyd

Lest We Forget

The legions of the lost, the dead and gone
Tears were shed for them by a loved one
They were young, stout-hearted and bold
Marching gallantly forward as they were told
On patriotic fervour and tumult their hearts took wing
Proudly onwards for regiment, country and king
But no mention was made of bullets and metal shred
The mud and gore, the wounded and mutilated dead
Brass bands and drums spoke only of victory and glory
But the truth, however, would tell a grimmer story
Tales of death and carnage, lost limbs and gas
Whole regiments decimated or slain en masse
Clambering from slimy rat infested trench lines
Across no man's land, through wire and mines
Into the hell of grenades and machine gun fire
Men ceased to exist in the lethal steel and mire
No trees grew, no birds sang, in that awful place
Only the black angel was present with smug face
A bountiful harvest was there for him to reap
For countless good men succumbed to permanent sleep
Now only rows and rows of crosses starkly signify
Where young, stout hearted men were finally to lie
Splashes of colour from poppy flowers, bright and red
God's own symbols of a nation's tragic war dead
Would this last resting place be one of peace
Or would the thunderous horror of war never cease.

John Keeling

Crafty Cat

Exit the cat,
Disdainful sniffs
And flicking tail
Scorning
The meaty morsels.
He will return
To human pleas,
And condescend
To eat roast pork.

Margaret Hawkins

The Awakening

The golden sun beats down on naked limb.
Flesh burns from the intensity of the invisible rays.
Without warning the wind strikes
fluttering up loosened cloth,
refreshing for a moment the sweltering form.
Then all at once sending a cold shudder down the spine.

Only a moment previously all had seemed blissful,
The warm tender touch of the sun mingled with gentle breeze,
inviting the prostrate form,
to slip back once again into dream.
For an instant deceived by the peaceful transition
from sleep to wakefulness.

Hidden in the darkness of the mind are pain and suffering,
unfulfilled hopes and desires of long ago,
enough to sadden the soul,
Yet the seed of possibility struggles,
to find a fertile place to propagate and grow.
But there is no where in the desolate blackness of the dream state.

Almost strangled, the spirit moves
to release the suffocating hold.
To liberate body and mind to wander in reality.
No longer constrained, able to rise
and take shelter in the shade.
Yet still experiencing the brilliance of life.

The seed of hope finds a place
to begin working out future possibilities.
Gone the desire to return to sleep
only the yearning to go forward into what is yet to come,
Embracing both the scorching nature of the sun
and the powerful force of the wind.

Jeanette Griffiths

Falklands Lament

This time we will and must therefore
Go out in a most defening roar,
No timid sound, no cry within,
No thought for our repenting sin,
For all our regrets have gone before,
We have let them out and closed the door,
Our memories of loved ones dear,
The ones that we now shed a tear,
For all our worldly good convey,
Material gained by us this day,
Left behind in our far off land,
Of whitened cliffs and golden sand,
What conflict will we unearth today,
On this lonely land so far away,
So come on lads, let's take the fight
and hope to see the morning light,
Let our loved ones not be sad,
As we prepare to leave Sir Galahad.

Graham Rutter

Advice

As you go through life
Some things must go wrong.
And the sooner you know it
           the better.
Believe in yourself.
Without growing too proud
And thank God for the beauty
           around you.
Forget the praise that falls
           to you
The moment you have won it.
Friendship is a chain of God
And all the world seems
           brighter?

So look on tomorrow, see flowers
           not weeds
And memories will always
           be bright,
The wisdom of ages if you read
           through the pages
Of this book and accept good
           advice.

Joan Ruddick

Lost

Lost, forgotten then found,
Quiet without a sound.
How, then I saw,
Hate without a war.
Loved, held then clean,
Sleep without a dream.
Future, past then here,
Things are never clear.
Light, all I saw was light,
The sky, the fields, the stream,
Bang, all I heard was bang,
Was this a horrid dream.
Smoke, all I smelt was smoke,
Black and grey and near,
Fire, all I saw was fire,
Things are never clear.

Lorna Jane Darby

These Dreams . . .

I have these dreams . . .

I take this heartache from my life;
It's just me and joy, hand in hand -
Sometimes turning and gliding
among things remembered . . .
My heart like a bird
Under a hopeful sun.

I run this fast,
Through elegant, young trees;
I am the measure of all things,
I am as a torn piece of cloud
Being blown by the wind,

. . . I have these dreams . . .

Leonard O'Hale

Tomorrow

Tomorrow I'll write a novel
Swim the channel
Climb a tree
Tomorrow I'll make a film
Talk to God
And stroke a bee
Tomorrow I'll do better
Bigger, taller things
Tomorrow I'll walk on water
Fight a fire
Grow some wings
While I'm waiting for tomorrow
I'll sit beside the sea
Until tomorrow comes
I think I'll just be me.

Rachel Fleming

Reminiscence

A village square, horse trough and clock.
Butcher, chemist and corner shop.
Church and chapel where people pray.
School, where children learn and play.
Quiet roads and narrow lanes.
Gardens reflected in window panes.
Fields where corn and poppies grow,
Blackberry and elder along the hedgerow.
New harvest now the fields do show,
Sprawling estates, houses row by row
Surround the church, and chapel too.
Large schools spread out and block the view.
Heavy laden lorries ply their way,
No village square is there today.
The roads are wide, to ease traffic flow,
Flashing lights tell when to go.
Cross that road, don't hesitate,
No time to stop and contemplate.
The days of peaceful sanity,
A village filled with tranquillity.

Sheila Farr

Scurrie the Squirrel

Scurrie the squirrel was always very busy
Just to watch him made me dizzy
He'd rush around the garden at a hundred miles an hour
Never pausing to see a pretty flower
He had one thing on his mind
To hide his food from animal kind
But alas the place he chose
Was just beneath my favourite rose
And now in the place where it should be
A sycamore stares back at me.

Caroline Nevile

Environment Friendly

Close your eyes, visualise the West Midlands, what can you see?
Perhaps leather saddlery, Sister Dora, Rainbow House, charity.
Markets, a bull ring, precious jewels, silver and gold.
Steps leading to Squares or Town Halls, decorous and old.
Ornate cathedrals, temples, mosques or museums of science.
Boulton and Watt and their steam-engine appliance.
Fine Gothic stone or Victorian brick, architecture restored to its
prime.
No longer concealed by a black shroud of historical grime.
Villages, towns with pedestrianised shopping precincts galore.
Art galleries, a Cadbury's chocolate factory, canals by the score.
Railways or roads like Spaghetti, that connect each great city.
The UCE, a motor car industry that's declining rapidly.
Traditional skills disappearing, engineering, keys and locks.
Homes with gardens and those in towering blocks.
The NEC arena and tradefairs that help boost the economy.
Foreign visitors exchanging greetings at meetings at the ICC.
A welcoming hand at hotels like 'The Hyatt' or the contrasting
'Grand'.
A BT tower, computer technology, Radio WM on the FM 95.6 band!
A magnificent Symphony Hall, with song and music resounding.
Barr Beacon with it's panoramic view equally outstanding.
Pigeons in churchyards, nature-centres with snakes,
Hanging baskets of flowers, parks full of lakes.
A wild bird sanctuary in the Sandwell Valley.
The beauty and grace of the 'Swan Lake' ballet.
Football fans sporting colours of the region's numerous clubs.
Local 'watering holes' the uninformed refer to as pubs!
Or perhaps unique individuals, each a small but integral part
Of community life, multiculturally rich, which beats at its heart.
Now open your eyes and you'll see, a born and bred Brummie
I consider to be, a privileged contemporary writer (with L plates) me!

Marilyn T Melvin

Modern View

It's not my problem the worlds decay
the miserable poverty will go away
if I look the other way.
Anyway the cost of beer is hard to pay
and my bosses yacht is rotting away.
I don't want to know.

The hole in the ozone is bigger they say,
as I drive my car down the motorway.
As I speed in a boat the Florida Keys,
As I take the kids for rainforest and fries.
What the sod do I care.

They say one day we'll have to pay
but the kids are happy munching away.
My beer's gone flat, all my problems are far away
The air in Greece is hot an sweet -
It's our third time here this year.
Saddam's been beat, if it's mad over there.
What the sod do I care.

His hands on the button, can they put him away?
It's not my problem world decay.
But the starving sods blame me.
They've nothing to lose, have they.
An icy wind is blowing my way.
The petrol ran out today.
My way of life is going away.
I'm on the toilet every day.
It is my problem now.

Dave Thompson

Alternative Spring

Matthew hibernated
Snuggled in the nest of self-pity
He (thought he) deserved.

Helen intruded
Filled his jam jars with flowers
She (knew he) adored.

A growing togetherness -
Walks through woods while sunlight chimes
Time's right (they believe) to love - again.

Georgina Clements

My Lover's Pen

Returning repentant to my lover's pen,
From my traitorous philosophies, my forbidden Zen.
Written thoughts not impressed,
Spoken words not addressed,
In my prodigal manner, I've come home to your nest.

My sweet paper child, these words that are yours,
Embossed on your heart are for no other cause,
Barr to banish your yearning,
Relieve you of weeps,
By whatever liquid my lover's pen seeps.

For your purest pale white, the faint lines that clothe you nude,
With whispering, guide my hands perform servitude.
So to you, my pen writes,
My wishful dream lover.
Not the first time, the last time, but not to another.

Jonathan Wood

Working

Working in the coal mines.
All day long.
Going home and sleeping all night.
Working by day.
Sleeping at night.
No time to enjoy the mysteries of life.
Bags under their eyes.
Hair withering away.
Bad bronchi cough
No life in those limbs.
Careless beings don't give a damn.
Their noses stuffed up with bits of grit
Faces are so black
Ears that don't hear
But the face is still active
Full of ideals and hope
That's all they really need.
To survive and work
In the coal mines
That's all they need.

Romesh Kaur

Balkans

Held in Tito's powerful grip
Europe's cockpit in simmering peace
Creeping westward mocking wealth
Rodina's errant child at play
Not quite east hardly west
A polyglot of ancient waring tribes
No Ferdinand this time to blame it on
Just old hates and changing boundary lines to battle on
Fleeting peace beyond all hope brushed aside like summer flies
Battles rage children die unimportant in the need to win
Starving people fleeing carnage ethnic cleansing what's it mean
Shells descend like monsoon rain reaping fear and death with pain
Profits rise some kept in work
Who cares what end they put them to
Not our business who they kill
Make them fast and sell them more
But don't show pictures on our screens
T'upsets the kids and shocks the wife.

Brian Hambleton

Untitled

If Jesus came to my church
I wonder what He would see
a church so antiquated
they still say thou and thee
or when He takes His seat
in worship and in prayer
I wonder . . . if He would hear
a voice say . . . 'That's my chair?'

If Jesus came to my church
I wonder what He would see
a church that's always busy
with meals and cups of tea
and socials in the evenings
and meetings every day . . .
the time goes by so quickly
there's no time left to pray

If Jesus came to my church
I wonder what He would see
compassion, love, kindness
or empty charity
The gossips and the whispers
of those bound down by sin
the moanings and the groanings . . .
who let those youngsters in!

John Masefield

Waiting for a Train

Waiting for a train;
A busy platform, people waiting to travel,
People ready to leave, waiting for a train;
A sunny afternoon, the sun beaming down,
Shadows of people, waiting for a train;
Trains come and go, people arrive and depart,
We sit still, waiting for a train;
Announcements over the tannoy, the 16.40 to Brighton,
But ours is delayed, waiting for a train,
That's run out of electricity, or lost its way,
The sun shines on, waiting for a train;
The sun sinks, the announcements continue,
Still we sit, waiting for a train;
People getting restless, people getting angry,
No end in sight, waiting for a train.
When, finally it happens,
Announcements over the tannoy,
For us no more
Waiting for a train.

Andrzej Rusyn

Honestly we Didn't

No, we didn't like Abba
we all sang
as the tune swam our heads
and we stashed the old 45's up in the loft
in case we were found out.

No, we didn't vote Tory
we all sang
as we crept to the ballot boxes
and put our X's next to little Johnny boy.
But at least Abba are fashionable now.

Matt Nunn

The Rain Drop

Precariously trembling on a leaf
Gold in sun and crystal clear,
Emanating colour, of autumnal bronze
Green cushioned, a rain-cloud's tear.

Sparkling like some precious jewel
Fools, the inquisitive jackdaw clown,
Cocks his head and in peculiar gait
Surveys the leaf with rain-drop crown.

Petals of roses in cascades falling
On the breeze with scented air,
About the ball of mirrored water
Faceting rose hued magic there.

A mysterious dance of preservation
The spider spins her silver thread,
She though supped the lovely bubble
Did not disturb it from its bed.

In all its splendour nestling there
Effect unnoticed in nature's course,
Did suddenly spill to soft brown earth
The very essence of all life's source.

Jo Rosson Gaskin

Lynmouth

Lovely Lynmouth in the spring
Lulled by water sound
From the constant torrents of the Lyn
And the mighty oceans pound

The year of fate in fifty two
A great wall of water swept
And the flood death toll grew and grew
And all of Lynmouth wept

Up through the trees to waters meet
Along wooded paths inclining
Passing flowers sweet in gardens neat
With hammocks for reclining

Behind the monkey puzzle tree
Of dark green gibbons tails
Extends a fine view out to sea
And the clear coast of distant Wales

Where 'Falls Point' slips to the sea
Bright eyed Jackdaws soar
And far below eternity
Lapping at the shore

Beyond the headland rising steep
Below a crown of silver cloud
A scattered flock of black faced sheep
Windswept in woollen shrouds

The storms have died without a trace
Or sign of Winter's trauma
Far across the moors the ponies race
In a wild springtime Gymkhana

K W Gittoes

The Fox

I saw a fox, once, in this field:
it paused, turned, stopped, just by the wood.
Stock-still then, the two of us stood
watching, as if for one to yield.
That was last spring. It's winter now.
Here I stand, as I did before,
perhaps to see the fox once more.
The cold earth lies bare. Not a bough
moves. Just one solitary sound -
the dismal cawing of a crow -
breaks the silence; and there is no
fox. Inexplicably, I've found
that moment in my memory
when fox-eyes fixed themselves on me.

Arthur McHugh

Mind Your Own Business

A young man, homeless, friendless
and out of work to boot;
all family and money gone;
no-one to care a hoot.

One evening on a London bridge
reflected in the Thames
about the plight of all like him
with neither home nor friends.

'Til finally, his morbid thoughts
enlarged the hump he'd got
and he decided that to jump
would end the blooming lot.

One of the world's do-gooders
was passing by that way,
and, summing the position up
thought he would have his say.

Persuaded the young man to hold
his horses for a time,
and listen to his argument
that life was really fine.

The man agreed; they talked awhile
each putting pros and cons,
and in the end, as you might guess
one of the two had won.

They stood, as if in parting,
and solemnly shook hands.
Both climbed onto the parapet
and jumped off hand-in-hand.

Tom Gibbons

Weights Room (Rap)

Strong men, carved out of African granite,
Employ muscles, extolling strength for virtue,
Soul mood in an inner-city weights room,
Machismo tuned, tuned to nature,
Increased volume, Rap and Ragamuffin,
Decrease tension of employment situation.

Fit men, strong men, yes, even hard,
Even harder to get a job if you're black!
Work those weights, pumping the iron,
Play the system, invert a raw deal,
For oneself, for dignity, for presence,
In a daytime, work-time, inner-city gym.

Reject the junk, the streets, the pub,
Clear the mind of, 'Blues' and tension,
No stigma employed here, only muscles employed here,
Hope and pray, erase the body's hypertension.
Don't separate the spirit from the flesh,
Work on different levels, vigilliantly, unilaterally.

Mind and body are one and whole
Strength of purpose - freedom goal,
No jobs. Lots of work! - resolution,
Forsee, then reap physical music, God like show,
From within oneself, high impact, anaerobic strength,
Laugh at status, purify the ego.

Richard Clarke

Friends Part One

My face expresses a pain
That she cannot wait to hear about
I reach into the smallest pocket of my 501's
Pass her the stone he gave me on Weymouth
                                            Beach

She smiles
'Romantic?' I say, nodding
'Pathetic!' she replies, laughing, eyes of
triangles the product of green and gold

Together we try to understand
why he hasn't 'phoned me

She explores every avenue
Totally positive
Even with jokes about a new girlfriend.

Sarah Milner

Thoughts on the Mysticism of Music - Confusion

The mind whirls and swirls in
Ever-increasing tangles and knots
Hopeless knots
Then the tangle that is the mind
Moves
I am able to stand back from it
Look, and observe
As if from beyond time
And there is music, a rock guitarist.

For a few precious minutes
I live for nothing else
It becomes easy, a flow
The mind is the music.

I realise then
I haved lived thru'
A whole lifetime of music, and
The mind, the music, the problem
Are all part of the pattern of existence.

Ankaret Shakti

Ghosts of Iron

Though the factories are silent,
And the steelworks are no more,
You can summon up the ghosts around
The foundry door.

You can feel the heavy beating
Of the great machines.
You will hear again the pumping,
Re-create the scenes.

If you listen you can hear them
Casting iron from the ore,
As they heat the rocks and charcoal
To the central core.

Hear the spitting and the hissing
Of the rushing steam,
The thumping and the thudding
Of the huge iron beam.

The roaring that is audible
For miles around,
As combustion melts ingredients
And sears the ground.

Now the trickling of the metal
As, unchecked, it flows,
And it sizzles from the outlet
Into pig-iron rows.

But the casting and the chaining
And the beating's done.
And the factories lie wasted
In the fading sun.

Gwyneth Theophilus

Separated

Darkness descends,
Blotting out all vision.
Existence continues in isolation.
Sounds have ceased,
Touch has terminated.
Everything centres on the soul.
Love exists in an isolation
Where time has stopped.
Nothing can now change me,
Nothing can impinge upon my soul
That has completed its destiny.
Now living in an empty world
With only memories of a perfect love -
A love removed from me.
I exist, waiting
For that eternal unison,
Yearning for the love that I once knew,
Wondering if only I exist
And you are gone forever from me.
Hoping, I wait.
That is all there is left to do -
To wait for my love,
To wait for you.

Susan J Allen

Listening

The golden thread of intuition,
Now we see it; now it's gone,
Stitching on through life's apparel,
Tenuously held as one.

Golden glimmers on the surface,
Knotty tangles underneath,
 - Referring to the pattern,
We'll learn what we bequeath.

Darting and diving needles,
Dolphins daring the prow,
Our straining and swerving ship
Sails the sea of life, somehow.

Winds of hope and lovely breezes
Softly tug the silken threads,
Shunned so often, in the bustle
Shaping thoughts inside our heads.

Knotty tangles, loops and snags,
Set to trip us in their snare,
Tease the golden thread right through it,
Simple know it, sew it - care.

We spin a thread of fantasy,
Lived from day to day:
We call it life - when we're awake,
But as we dream - we hear the way.

Brenda Dove

Anthem for Today's Agnostic

When asked, 'Do you believe?'
I look to our inheritance.
Seeing only man's fire that ravages the land
And the barbed wire fences built by his hand.
Mindless destruction for constructions sake
Leaving nature to drown in its polluted wake.

When told to, 'Trust in Him'
I ask those who have.
Dying in the desert to which they were lead
Or the lifeless body on a concentration camp bed
Withering in cells from an unwilling fast
Like the countless victims betrayed in the past.

When urged to 'Confess all Sin'
I seek the source.
Finding only empty refuse cans
And vacant eyes that fear to stare
At the crumbling stone scenery
In this lonely back-street lair.

When invited to, 'Join in Praise'
I fail to see why.
As children lie starving when crops feel no rain
While millions are lost when war rages again
But lazy harvest mice grow fat and old
Living in temples in sacrificed gold.

Ian Buckingham

Untitled

Someone has left;
they are speeding to another town.

The garden burns;
a fierce unnatural sun beats down.

The rush of pain
Is not for this departing only;
it gathers in
the older grief that made you lonely.

The sun abates;
its fires have almost ceased their raging.

The grass has cooled . . .

E F Scott

All in my Head

Hello, it's me
You remember me
You never showed, at the library I mean
You said you would
I needed you
I just needed to see your face
Joke, talk, visit reality, normality.
You didn't show
You left me alone - inside my head
With all its weird imaginings
I think I am going slowly, painfully mad
I'm not over dramatising
I'm facing what will soon be my reality
That's just it you see
I'm losing a tenuous grip on reality
I'm sliding further and further into my own world and
                                                    fancies.

Don't worry, it's not too painful
It's easy if you don't fight
Soothing, relaxing, it's like going home.
No-one can hurt you, no-one can reach you
All I want is to be alone
Somewhere where I won't have to face people, situations,
                                                    feelings

Somewhere where there are no confrontations
No families, no guilt, no self-inflicted pain and hatred . . .
In my head I can hear your voice telling me to grow
                                                    up.

To stop being selfish
I can see your face not understanding - forget it I'm just
                                                    babbling

I'll change the subject and talk about tomorrow
While in my head any reason I possess
Drowns in an ancient blue sorrow.

Saba Zai

Questions

Why are they called 'Sports fans'
When they can't abide by the rules
And make up their own?

Why are they called 'Joyriders'
When they bring grief and misery
Caused by their bravado?

Why are they called freedom fighters
When they take it away
From innocent bystanders?

Why are they called our representatives
When the people's views aren't considered
And we feel frustration?

Maybe one day common sense will prevail
With sportsmanship the competitor's aim
The car will be used for pleasure not pain
Ah for those sweet summer days once again
When the world was at peace with itself.

Betty Hall

Pipe Dreams

My wife and I are well-to-do,
With two lovely kiddies,
Plus a cottage with a view;
A garden full of fruit and flowers -
Two cats, two dogs and two cars.
So I should be a happy man
And should, with every passion bless
These joyful days of happiness.
> Yet . . . somewhere in my inner mind
> I have longings of another kind.

In reverie I see so plain
With scenic clarity
Brilliant sunshine, palm trees swaying
And waving on a golden beach.
And near, within easy reach,
In imagination I see
Bronzed maidens with inviting lips,
Flashing eyes and beguiling hips.
> Pure fantasy I realise
> But . . . It's fun to dream of paradise.

John Castel-Nuovo

Armchair Traveller

The old woman, tied to her chair by pain,
Gazes out at the Midlands rain,
But in her mind's eye, she can see the crest,
The mighty towers of Everest.

She sits and stirs in her hard wooden chair,
Smelling the damp and the fume-filled air,
But in her ears are the splash and the dip
Of porpoises larking as they follow her ship.

She sits and waits to be put to bed,
But the pictures continue the show in her head,
And as she snugs the shawl round her arms
She can feel the swaying of coconut palms.

She stretches her limbs and flexes her back,
Peers at the wallpaper's splintering crack,
But inwardly, as the one bar glows,
She is viewing the splendours of eternal snows.

Ruth Parker

To Louis

My first grandson, on the day you were born
The day was bright, the sun shone warm
As I gazed upon your tiny form
I swore to be your friend.

I know at times, the way is long
And hard on the shoulders of one so young
But I'm one who knows and can speak the tongue
The language of a friend

No matter what fate life has in store
In my heart there's always an open door
And I'll be there for evermore
Always to be your friend

And when the day comes, as come it will
I'm no longer here, there's a place to fill
I'll walk beside you, if that's God's will
Remember me as a friend.

John Carter-Dolman

Untitled

I had told myself the biggest lie, one I really did believe,
Have now erased the lie I told and the truth, at last, perceive.
Had said I held no hatred, no bitterness, no hurt,
but once the lie was swept away found those emotions in the dirt.
And then! And then! I wept, I wailed at what's been done to me,
lost memories now bombard my mind now free from tyranny.
My best friend tells me of the wrong that I mistook for right,
he gave emotions back to me lost long in my night of fright.
Expression first of long lost hate then hot anger burned my face,
my hands were clenched like fists of iron to punch the long years of
disgrace.
'Not me! Not me! 'twas never me,' wept the good girl so long hid,
then screamed the feelings so long gone 'til all released and can
forgive.
Can identify emotions, in restraint no longer bound,
'tis good health to have these feelings, tho' intense when first they're
found.
Have already learned the difference, preferring happiness to hate,
Happy is a rainbow bubble whilst hate, a heavy weight,
and love is warm and wonderful and bitterness icy cold.
Love is all enfolding, bitterness too cold to hold.
My Lord teaches me the difference and shows me what is best -
I *shall* keep the best emotions and discard the rubbish rest . . .

of course!

Rosie Hues

176

Tara

Tara, Tara, you are my best friend
We walked the lanes together
Thinking this would never end
You were only a baby when we first met
I held you and loved you and gave you my heart
Our life was good and wonderful
And then we had to part

The years flew by so quickly
The seasons come and go
Oh Tara, Tara how I feel
You'll never never know

I never had a friend like you
I never will again
Even though others will take your place
It will never be the same

The time had come for you to go
I held you close to me
I looked into your tired face
Your eyes as always true
You passed into another world
Another time and place
But one thing always stays with me
My friend your loving face

We loved each other, always true
My friend, my dog, I still love you.

Mary F Barratt

Meditation

I breathe,
And peace comes.
Here in my room I receive
the peace of mountains, forests
And lakes.

I breathe,
Beyond the music others
play, I hear the silence
of space and stars
That is inside me.

I breathe,
There is no time, no
space, yet all time and
All space.

I continue with my daily
life -
Refreshed.

Jane Edwards

Petrified Fantasy of the Covenant Tree

Priest-wish for the dance of the Giant's to start;
Stand to watch them, daydreams from one's own heart,
As the scene floats: flight of the Hanging Stone,
Circular expression, caught horizon,
Whirling sun, plausible blue stone - think!
Little axe, little dagger, sword from lake;
This, the round table, those knights of stone take
On the star scene, the ley line, the slaughter,
Ransom and fall to earth daughter:

> Looking at the sky, thinking of you,
> Dreaming of breaking the protective blue
> Around your body; plunge to your heart:
> Blood-warm shimmer in your eyes
> Like glowing fullness of your voice.
> Oh! the flames we put our hands into,
> Without selfish thought, to grasp the essence
> Imagined to relieve ignorance!

Merlin trapped, hidden under rock,
Wizened wizard less wise led to the shock.
Guinevere's beauty betraying the quest;
Morgana's magic forming treacherous test.
Quiet in the plain, a key without lock.

So, will future sons see skeletal forms
Of old factories; keyless, rusted locks
And will the operators - spiritless storms -
Flounder? Could England lose brave-heart spirit?
We're waiting like Merlin to break through rock.
Sometimes it's hard to hope yet self-denial to submit.

Suzanne Stratful

I Used to Talk to the Moon

When I was a boy
I used to talk to the moon
In the early evening of a cold, clear winter's day
On my way home from school
I'd tightrope walk along a wall
And tell him all I knew

Now that I'm older
The magic is gone
I no longer talk to the moon
My eyes look down
My head
No longer amongst the stars.

P M Holloway

The Church

There's a little church in Huntington,
To the west of Tackeroo.
You'll find it on the main A34.
It's out of Cannock - just a bit,
Straight on past the local pit -
For half a mile, and then you're at the door.

It's been there for donkey's years,
And the people had their fears
A time or two, that it might have to close.
But they always firmly trusted
That the church would not be busted,
That growth would come - and that is what God chose.

For that growth has come at last,
And for several years past
The church has slowly flourished, found its feet.
There's always something doing,
There's always something brewing -
All sorts of things - where folk in fellowship can meet.

There's still much to do, of course,
But, with God the driving force,
It's a place where you can go and always find
A quiet time for prayer;
The word of God to share -
Thoughtfulness, and gentle peace of mind.

There's a little church in Huntington,
St. Thomas' is its name.
It's withstood the test of time, as we can see.
Its doors are open wide -
There's lots of room inside,
And a welcome always there for you and me.

Stan Shaw

Childhood

One sunny afternoon in Spring
I came across some children at play,
And among the shouts of gladness
My memory transported me to another day.

I saw myself through the eyes of a boy
And cast aside my mask of manhood,
And with a tear of joy
Embraced the child in my heart.

Robert J Goodall

To be a Child at Christmas

You wake up Christmas morning,
And look out at the snow.
Though you don't always find it,
The day has got a glow.
You go out on the landing,
Oh listen to the din.
The children have their presents,
You know that Santa's been.
The children all come running,
To show you what they've had.
There's clockwork trains and baby dolls,
And a football for the lad.
There's lots of lovely presents,
And of course a bike, a pram.
A teddy bear, a spotty dog,
A lovely book for gran.
You hurry down for breakfast,
The day has just begun.
You wish you were a child again,
And could have all the fun.

B Hope

Trees in the Four Seasons

I love the trees in their new spring green
And walking on the new grass that has just been mown
The sight of the trees and smell of the grass
What more in life could anyone ask

In summer the trees although still green
Have a look about them that is not so serene
And beginning to droop as autumn draws near
But still it's a wonderful time of the year

Now it's autumn what a beautiful sight
The trees in their colours of yellow red and gold
Standing there brightly as well they might
For it is indeed a wonderful sight

Spring summer and autumn have gone
Now winter has come
And the trees cast their shadows on fallen snow
But it is still a wonderful sight you know

The poplar stands tall like a finger pointing to the sky
Saying come on spring you know you are nigh
And when it comes we know we will see
The lovely spring green on the wonderful tree.

Nellie Ellis

A Beautiful Dream

To sleep, to float away on a dream,
For peace upon the earth, t'would be supreme.

For in my dream there's no war, no hostility,
'Tis a dream of joy, peace and tranquillity.

A beautiful dream, there's no more sin,
A wondrous dream, of no more famine.

For many my dream may seem to be vague,
But there's no more sickness, or plague.

You may well ask will my dream come true;
Well my friend, I leave that to you.

I suppose my dream seems somewhat obscure,
In this world, where everything is unsure.

Please forgive this man's beautiful dreams,
For, alas that's all they are, so it seems.

In a world where only love does reign,
In such a world there's no more pain.

In my dream world no more death or dying,
For in my beautiful dream, no more crying.

In this modern world of great futility,
There seems little room for any humility.

J Felton

Mid Stream

'There's nowhere to go and nothing to do,'
Lamented young Johnny while sat on the loo.
'Come here this instant,' his mum did declare.
'There are plenty of places to go anywhere.
We'll start with the gardens and cycle the paths,
Manifold Valley . . . the swimming baths.
Chatsworth and Rudyard, Biddulph and Bakewell,
Cheddleton Railway, the Tittesworth trail,
The Bass museum . . . Hartington way.
At Chatterly Whitfield we'll spend a day,
Look over Bridgemere then on to the moors.
Visit the Mills, hear all the folk lores . . .
Coombes valley, Froghall, Matlock, Consall.
Plus Alton Towers where you'll have a ball . . .
Walking and fishing, climbing and sitting,
Three Shires Head is ideally befitting.
Farm Park at Ipstones, Bird World at Winkhill,
Sit on canal bank to picnic at will . . .
Markets at Ashbourne, Cheadle and Leek,
Amidst all the wonders of countryside *peak* . . .
There are so many places where you can go
And so many things you can do.
So get off your backside and start making tracks,
You're never too young to digest all the facts . . .
It's on everyone's doorstep to enjoy and admire,
So get out those bikes and pump up my tyre . . . '

Margarette L Damsell

Value of Eyesight

We all should value our eyesight,
Much more than we do.
One of our most precious possessions
That has ever been given to you.

Most of our gifts are taken for granted,
Because they were given us free.
Where developed by human nature,
This was always our necessity.

So we in our way of living,
Should always take more care
Of the greatest treasure we hold,
For appreciation always in our prayers.

How we can aid our eyesight,
Give our eyes plenty of rest.
Never overstrain them,
If need be take a test.

If you really need glasses
To help and ease the strain,
Make quite sure you use them,
Don't forget this old refrain.

Harold Willmott